CLASS ACTION

Making the Future W

Dian Cohen and Guy Stanley

ROBERT DAVIES PUBLISHING
MONTREAL / TORONTO

Distributed in Canada by

Stewart House,
380 Esna Park Drive
Markham, ON L3R 1H5

☎ (Ontario & Quebec)1-800-268-5707
☎ (Rest of Canada) 1-800-268-5742

FAX 1-905-940-8864

ISBN 1-895854-22-9
1   2   3   4   5   93   94

Acknowledgements

Thanks to Guy's HEC colleagues, especially Alain Noel and Fernand Amesse, and the University of Toronto's Alan Rugman, from whose conversations and presentations about these matters he has benefitted enormously. Dian expresses her particular appreciation for the insights gained in conversation with Canadian business managers and NGO executives.

A number of federal and provincial public servants also contributed in various ways, as always, to helping us understand the world. Thanks, too, to Tom Barnes, who designed and laid out these pages. The conclusions expressed therein, however, are ours alone, as is responsibility for any errors.

CANADA, AUTUMN, 1993

Dedication

To the children

Table of Contents

Introduction

Among the least comforting and most worrying discussions that are held both publicly and privately are those about debts and deficits, interest rates, taxes and constitutions, and the future of life as we know it in Canada. We've taken part in these discussions, we've written a book about possible solutions to these big issues, we've read and listened to the views of others on these subjects. And then we began to wonder whether there wasn't something else we could do to improve our situation, something smaller in scope, easier to implement, something that might provide us all with an economic and political comfort zone.

We came up with a book about possibilities: about the changes that are already ongoing in the economy, changes that point the way forward and introduce new elements into the discussion of how to overcome our economic difficulties. We think it will help you benefit from economic change and maybe even find your own "comfort zone" within the colossal shifts taking place in the way we work, the way we govern ourselves and the way we connect to the world around us.

Even as Canadians struggle to understand the basic nature of an "information-based" economy, evidence of how different it is from an industrially-based one inexorably piles up. Example: "traditional" forecasting methods indicate that the economy has been in recovery mode for the last year and is now growing again. But it has happened without an accompanying spurt in job creation, partly because the other indications of growth (increasing spending, rising inflation etc.) are absent. And even though many of us can't yet see the whole picture, we can cite examples in our own lives of where the differences have touched us. We wonder, for example, where we'll work if we lose our jobs. We wonder about what changes we have to make just to keep them. And with technology changing so fast, we wonder, even if we make the changes, the jobs will continue to exist.

U nderlying our concerns is a dramatic economic revolution, a profound change in the material base of society generally referred to as the structural change from an industrial to an information economy. There's been lots of discussion about that change at a general level. *Less discussed is what's happening at the micro level of the economy, at the level of the firm where most people actually work or want to work.*

Yet something interesting and exciting is taking shape in the new world out there — a new organizational form that analysts have alluded to as "flattening the management curve". That's jargon for companies streamlining themselves by taking out layers of management and emerging as much leaner, flatter structures. But that's only the tip of the iceberg of transformation the private sector is undergoing. What's replacing organizations characterized by management hierarchies —so-called "silo" organizations— is a production structure based on networks — a web of specialists and complementary abilities interconnected by superfast information links.

Throughout the private sector signs of networked organizations are everywhere: from banking, to retail stores, to company-supplier relations, to the way goods move around the world. In essence, the walls that divided organizations from each other in the industrial world are tumbling down and new, information-sharing, permeable organizations are emerging.

The contrast is particularly startling when compared to the public sector, that is, government and other tax-supported institutions like schools and universities, hospitals and crown corporations. For the public sector—despite some investment in this area—has not yet made the same kinds of changes. The public sector represents about 40 per cent of national economic activity and creates the environment within which the private sector operates. Arguably, the public sector's resistance to changing itself is THE major problem in Canada's economy. Unfortunately, the shift to a global economy that works through interlinked networks poses enormous problems for governments and the assumptions on which they are based. Among the major challenges:

Macro-economically, Canada is both strapped and trapped. The debt's so large, we have to keep borrowing to finance it, so it grows larger. Taxes are so high now, raising them more would actually reduce revenue. Cutting taxes would stimulate the economy, but likely not enough to offset the additional borrowing. Interest rates are at historical bottoms now; any upward movement would only make things worse. Canadian borrowers still pay more than those in the US anyway, partly because to most observers a dose of inflation looks like the easiest way out. The alternative is to focus on the micro-economy which is changing dynamically. That's the course we advocate here.

- The shift to networked organizations accelerates the power shift from top to bottom. It challenges the rationale for governments organized in departments and ministries, the meaning of government programs and service to the public;

- The change to internationally linked networks as the economy's production units accelerates the shift away from national, or macro, economies, to micro economies. *And it changes the focus of micro economics from the firm to the network. Taken together these shifts mean that effective economic policy has to be micro policy, not macro policy.* Macro policy cannot on its own return Canada to economic health.

Only a focus on micro policy can provide the policies we need to cure the deficit and debt problems, and move the country back to fat times and money sandwiches. That means a focus on helping networks work better.

Throughout this book, we develop these themes, illustrating the private sector changes and showing how a focus on networks spotlights areas where micro-policy can produce dramatic advances. There are lots of small, specific changes we could make right now that would take the economic phasers off stun and move us into warp speed.

Canadians are already paying a price for economic failure and the failure of adjustments in public life to match or even lead private sector change. If we are to lead or even match, we must deal with the world as it is, and fix what's possible to fix.

Here's what we have to do:

1. Understand that things have changed: if we do that, we can write an agenda for doing what's possible to do, rather than trying to resist change and preserve the past. This means, above all, reorganizing the way government works.

2. Use our imaginations and the technology already available today. The newly emerging organization form, the network, can provide the best vehicle for adaptation.

  - For instance, we can help sew up the tears in the social fabric by shifting tax points to the cities, not provinces.

  - We can accelerate networked education and the use of computers as "knowledge engines" by putting phone jacks in the classroom and taking advantage of the networks that already exist.

  - We can use existing business networks like Interac (the one you use with your bank card) to break down job market/training stickiness — after all, jobs ARE economic artifacts, so let's treat them as such, not as a branch of social policy.

  - We can slash the nation's staggering paper burden with up-to-date document management strategies.

  - We can fund urban "freenets" (like those in Ottawa and Victoria) so communities can network themselves and, through Internet, be in touch with the rest of the world.

Internet is the world's largest computer network. This alone would be a huge boost for small business, where the new economy is being created.

- We can remove barriers to entrepreneurship by loosening up financial services, and changing telecommunications policy to promote competition and new services, based on helping people, not serving producer interests.

- We can provide instant write-offs of new technology.

What's in it for people who want to work? More work, because it will be easier to create jobs, easier to tap into international markets, easier to hook the Canadian imagination up to the world.

The election campaign winners pledged a $6 billion public works program to promote growth and jobs. The key idea was that once the people saw the trucks moving, they'd feel the economic stimulus was effective. But today's trucks are linked by satellite so they can change their routes as conditions change; the goods they carry are controlled and paid for through computer links and designed and manufactured by exchanges across other networks. The most effective way to get the trucks moving is not more concrete and lanes (although more north-south highways are imperative). It's more transmission bandwidth or carrying capacity, more telecom services, more telecom switches that can handle huge data bursts and lower phone rates — which simply will not happen if we settle for a clutch of 1930s-style make-work projects.

The discomfort we feel is often portrayed as a consequence of adjustment to globalization, free trade and technological change. This book argues the contrary: failure to adjust, insurmountable obstacles to change, and a political system that no longer does the job are causing this pain. We are losing our middle class and sapping the confidence of Canadians in their future. Standard democratic reaction: Throw the bums out AND change the institutions. Canadian voters accomplished the first on October 25, 1993. But nobody in the campaign offered us the second — institutional changes —except in terms of (again!) the constitution.

Virtually all the new federal parliament is composed of people who are either new to power or haven't touched power since the rules of the game changed in the mid-1980s. So a change in people won't matter much if they don't understand what's wrong with the system they're supposed to fix. Our system may still have the capacity to reenergize itself, but only if the team using it has already passed its drivers' ed course. So think of this book as an update of the car driver's handbook. And wish the new drivers well. We can't afford many more mistakes at the wheel.

2

Not "Just The Economy, Stupid" . . .

As Adam said to Eve on leaving the Garden of Eden,

> **"My dear, we're living in an age of transition."**

Today's transitions are generally discussed in terms of changing economic outputs, but a more helpful approach is to look at shifting forms of organization and the implications for the underlying social fabric.

That's what this chapter is about.

. . . Organization Matters

From the huge government department, to the large corporation, to the big hospital, many big, vertical entities are fast finding themselves without life support systems. To survive, private corporations are rapidly transforming themselves into flatter, more customer-driven, networked organizations. So far, public sector gargantua are generally failing to match these changes, although their financial oxygen supply is also being constricted.

Why is this happening? In our previous book, *No Small Change* (MacMillan, 1993), we pointed out the logic of the information revolution. That is, it vastly lowers the cost of information. Today, an individual equipped with a computer, a modem, the appropriate software and from $200 to $1,000 for research, can in a few hours amass and analyze as much useful data on any subject as a government department or a corporate research department could in a week. If that information is then posted on an electronic bulletin board where it is examined, clarified, added to etc. by others in a like-minded network, you can in effect mobilize action in a few hours that previously took months and months of preparation.

The technology is only one aspect of these changes. Another is the way competition changes the rules of the game. A great deal has already been written about companies, documenting evidence that as the computer revolution progresses, companies are realizing that they have to stick to what they know best and where they can add value most effectively. Otherwise, their weaker elements will drag them down competitively, as other companies, focusing on these elements of their business, force them out.

Over the last eight years or so, business has found out, sometimes painfully, the kind of organizational forms that allows them to compete effectively in this witheringly tough environment. They have begun the move from hierarchies to networks. Organizations that were once tall and self-isolated from their environment, with information flowing uphill and power downhill — corporations — are morphing with radical speed into networks. As these changes become more widespread, society is changing, too. From a society that organized production through big corporations, we are becoming a society in which the main work is now done in networks.

The model is no longer a portfolio of enterprises run by a "big picture" staff adding value through centralized procedures. Today's successful companies are client-servers in a network composed of key suppliers, key customers and the transformation process. Many, many activities that were once accomplished within the company walls are now entirely or partly externalized to sub-contractors who understand and share company values and procedures but are more or less outside the formal company structure—like cousins in a family. The company acts as a client, server, and private branch exchange (PBX) — a sophisticated switch among the different elements of the business. That way companies can get the same product or services at in-house quality or better, but for much less money and on a pay-as-you-go basis. Other benefits include faster time to markets and no inventory pile-ups. Where these evolve into a two-way arrangement of clients and servers, suppliers also get instant world-wide access to global markets through the big companies' own international networks. Applied across a country, the

**"Client-server"
technology** is the name for networks of individual work stations and personal computers. In the mid-'70s, deregulation and decentralization, coupledwith the need for quality and efficiency improvements created a demand for computerized information systems to help organizations cope. If you've ever tried to decide on a PC and peripherals, you know the bewildering variety of hardware and software to choose from. Hence a market- driven demand for a new kind of consultant — the systems integrator.

A Systems Integrator helps customers decide how computers can help them, selects and installs the right hardware and software to do the job, and teaches their customers how to use it. Most corporate information systems of the 1970s ran on giant mainframe computers locked in climate-controlled rooms and maintained by white-coated experts. Mainframe companies that installed these systems, like Andersen Consulting, IBM and Electronic Data Systems (founded by U.S. presidential candidate Ross Perot) got rich.

By the late 1980s, another revolution was under way. The stunning decline in the cost of computer hardware, matched by vastly increasing processing power and memory, meant that systems once restricted to mainframes could be moved on to desktop computers. These more nimble systems linked work stations and personal computers; they could be fine tuned more precisely to fit the needs of specific business operations.

Such "client-server" networks can be built faster and with smaller hardware budgets than mainframe systems, but they're even more complex to design and operate. A typical network may connect some 40 different products and require fewer but more highly trained systems integration experts to put it all together.

*From the files of The Globe &
Mail **Report on Business
Magazine** (hereafter referred
to as ROB)*

networking of companies is rapidly becoming the networking of our material life.

Can't government use these techniques? Of course they can. But first they have to forget their current idea of a department. A department still runs on the myth that all power comes from the crown. Therefore, it's set up as a vertically arranged group of people with an allegedly all-knowing or all-coordinating deputy minister at the top and cascading authority down to the analyst who actually works the file. The analyst could do it all and pass the data directly to the minister for decision. But in our governments, there has to be three or four layers of potential nay-sayers and critics in between. So information that would take an individual a couple of hours to develop takes a department days, weeks, months — depending on its urgency and how controversial it is. That's because analysts still have to pass the information up and down the vertical authority before they can decide what do with it. Flattening the organization to two layers—analyst and minister—would, however, call into question the very idea of a government ministry or department. Moreover, networks are very level playing fields on which people communicate as peer to peer—and they expand access. Organizations based on the formula "Access equals Power", with strong rank consciousness would have an especially hard time restructuring themselves into networks. Why? Because that kind of reorganization is frightening to too many people.

A network doesn't have very many authority stacks — chains of command by which increasingly costly or strategic decisions are taken as you move up the chain. Instead, it's multinodal, like a market. Instead of linear and phased, it is non-linear and simultaneous. Instead of being closed to outside participation, it is open to outsiders, on a reciprocal basis (but if you don't share, too, you get left out.)

Think of it this way: just like rocks break scissors, networks beat hierarchies. Private sector organizations are discovering this daily, although the progress to date has taken the better part of a decade and vertical departments still exist. The public sector has made almost no inroads on the new organization form. (Although, to be fair, more and more government *information products* are appearing on electronic networks.) Government is still made up of vertical departments trading access as a commodity. Breaking down hierarchy and using networks would end duplication, speed turnaround time and slash costs, as it has for the private sector.

In contrast to steeply vertical organizations in which big decisions are taken by bigshots, networks facilitate its members in taking many individual decisions. In small networks, participants may adhere to some collective agenda. But today's big computer networks like Internet and Bitnet are totally decentralized, of unknown dimension and as polymorphous as a city, with millions of members. They enable people to inform themselves, to communicate with other people, to share and shape things of common interest, and to ignore what doesn't interest them.

These networks are not anarchistic: there are rules and most people abide by them. The rules are more like conventions and traffic regulations. Essentially, each electronic bulletin board has its conventions, and to improve the quality of its own networking, it will adjust the rules as it goes along.

Most people on networks are looking for something: mainly new tools to make their lives more fun or more convenient. Suppliers offer their products on these networks in an arrangement known as shareware. You can download a pretty good working model of the program free. Then if you use it and like it, you're obligated to pay for it. Shareware's growing phenomenally. Many of the world's best selling software programs have started out as shareware and are now multi-million dollar businesses. Shareware is one of the most innovative and interesting developments of the information age. For it combines many of the attributes of a traded good (you get what you pay for) with a "free" benefit that others subsidize. Amazingly, in light of conventional economics, people do pay for shareware. They want to show their appreciation of the product and the value added they have received. They want to receive the additional features of the program not included in shareware versions. And they want to be part of the network of preferred customers who are automatically informed of updates with the opportunity to upgrade at modest increments to the initial purchase and registration fee.

The Network Close Up

Let's look a little more closely at this new organizational form, the network. It's value is based on being open and accessible. The more people it links, the more it's worth. Compuserve now has a million members. Prodigy has a similar number. The Internet may have anywhere from five to 13 times that. One of its half dozen or so file transfer systems from only one address or node on the network recently reached 97,000 files transmitted a day.

Like a phone circuit, the value of these networks comes from the amount of contact you have with other people. There's another value, too: the variety of things you can do, the applications. This is what gives these networks their bazaar-like quality. The more participants in a network, the greater its attractiveness to me, a supplier of applications, and vice versa.

A network's value grows with its extensiveness, its inclusiveness. A network is the opposite of a club. The value of a club membership is a function of its exclusivity. If anyone can join a club, what's the point?

Our political structures — public and private — are more like clubs than networks. They're built on exclusivity that derives from access to a central decision-maker. If you've got access to the president/prime minister etc., you're more important than someone who has not. Political lobbying, the pecking order in a government department, etc., all depend on access to the central decision-maker — like a hive in which the bees around the queen are the core, and the workers are just programmed to get on with their jobs.

As mentioned earlier, a traditional, many-layered hierarchical private company is not much different: the CEO is the central decision-maker and so all power flows from him. A major issue in corporate governance just now is how to make that power more accountable to shareholders, just as voters want to know how to make political power more accountable to them.

Our point is that these organizations are all outmoded. Microsoft got to be valued as much as General Motors — despite the fact that in terms of assets and sales it's only about one tenth the size — because its president, Bill Gates, understood the economics of networks. Why is Microsoft's DOS the top computer operating system? Because it opened up its system to applications writers from the beginning. Since there were more off-the-shelf applications for DOS than its competitors, voila! Open architecture that permits anyone interested to participate automatically guarantees added value over a closed and proprietary network.

The implications for government are more profound than you might think. Historically, all democratically elected political power, from the Reform Bill of 1832 to our own day, is based on clubs, not networks.

A club — or cabal or political party — takes power, denying it to others, and uses that power to reward its friends. Power thus becomes a commodity to be bought and sold: accountability between elections virtually nil. Thus, between elections politicians are able to "exercise leadership" — that is, act unilaterally — in ways that they will not exercise closer to elections. Hence, too, the election budget practice of bribing the taxpayer with his own money.

Only the collapse of the fisc (i.e. the failure of government to pay for itself) has called this historic form of politics into question. As, equally, the collapse of the fisc called the divine right of kings into question several hundred years ago. But if power can't be based on clubs, can it be based on networks?

S uperficially, there are many reasons to doubt it can. Power issues commands which must be obeyed. Obedience promotes change in the direction desired by the powerful. Power DOES depend on club-like relations. Diffused power cannot command, it can only coordinate and facilitate. Cooperation, not obedience, promotes change in the direction desired, reflecting a general decision, not a centralized one. Surely, when it comes down to a contest, a well- run club will beat a diffuse network every time, will it not?.

Well, if that were true, why does a networked firm outperform a centralized stand-alone firm every time?

Why does General Electric use a network to provide instant readings on world wide products? Why are supermarkets transforming themselves into networked nodes between suppliers and customers with new, more attractive pricing for the customer? What's more, remember, these networks work not because of some oversight power but in spite of power and lawyers — networks operate because they are self-enforcing bargains.

Except for the technology part, there is nothing especially new about the advantages of networks. A clear example, unfortunately one too little known except by historians, is the role played by just such arrangements in the industrialization of England. This example is illustrative of the fact that it is relationships — not just technology — that really matter. The example: the 18th century English clearing houses, which were able to settle accounts throughout the country on a daily basis and thereby make the financing of companies much easier in England than elsewhere at that time. Also, the extensive, cooperative network raised the volume of transactions, making the financing more profitable for everyone.

Can We Move To Networks?

So what's the bottom line for government? It really boils down to this: Can Canada's social fabric, now so heavily clubbed, be easily networked?

Actually, it's happening already. And not just in Canada, but throughout North America. Some cases in point, already occurring in public and private sector applications, but by no means an exhaustive list:

- **urban freenets** in Ottawa, Victoria, Cleveland and elsewhere. These urban bulletin boards promote discussion, sharing, joke-writing, and mutual counsel. They also help small business. Above all, they make borders permeable and thus make the institutions that order our lives more malleable. Networks allow services to customize themselves at the pace of the user.
- **political e-mail.** Compuserve has had its Congressgram application for some years now. Bill Clinton is the first US president to make White House briefings and other material automatically available on request via e-mail; Canadian government press releases are listed on some services by department.
- **on-line brokerage**. This allows people to do their own stock market research, make their own investments, and in many ways take on the institutions through computing capacity. There is still too much opacity in the North American investment game, but the trends are for making this work even more effectively.
- **on-line banking**. This allows anyone to move her/his balances around and pay bills without having to go to the bank; it thus complements the direct payment

plans of many companies. Only outmoded regulations prevents us from making full use of this system's existing capabilities.

● on-line news, research and other information, including "forums" of like-minded people, counseling each other.

These networks are to information what the 18th century clearing house was to money. Then, money was the constraint on growth. Today, — it's ideas, concepts, knowledge and the ability to apply it to improving lives that are the constraints on growth. For instance, want some ideas on how to improve your company's cash flow or take into account a particular tax measure? Try looking up the "Accounting and Tax, Library 9", in the Working from Home Forum files on Compuserve (Go Work) These network organizations alleviate that constraint and help power economic growth. Trouble is, finding Canadian applications can be difficult.

If the wealth of nations in the 18th century was based on access to capital, and in the 19th century it was based on access to machinery, then in the late 20th, it's based on **access to knowledge**.

The effect of networks — in a nutshell — is to cut out intermediaries and make it easier to pay as you go, learn as you go, etc. Economically, it means that citizens can shift their investments almost as fast as institutional investors, thus equalizing the balance a little. Politically, it means that concerned citizens can patrol the news agencies and make sure the politician's office sees clips and items his departmental handlers could keep from him. It means that protests can instantly be delivered to government leaders and corporate CEOs. Examples of networks that have effectively changed government priorities: environmental activists and women's groups, fax news services and e-mail that helped block the 1992 Soviet coup against democratization, and Faxnet that put the heat on Chinese authorities during the events leading up to Tiannemen Square.

Networking works both ways, too: leaders who can use this technology to regularly poll the public, can find out what people think more easily than those who have to rely exclusively on surveys and poll captains. Plus they can develop personal relationships with voters that go beyond what a constituency mailer could achieve.

What's the end of this process going to look like? More participation does not necessarily mean better decisions. But what we are now seeing and will continue to see is a gradual submergence of club power into networks. Accompanying this trend will be the progressive de-legitimizing of club power, so that sudden decisions made to allocate rewards without some form of public approval — such as the last government's decision to spend $5 billion on new helicopters without a foreign and defence policy review, or patronage appointments — will incur increasing network disapproval. Indeed, networks can be used to bypass the old-boys club and open wide the candidature for public appointments.

As for government departments, they will have to become more like networks and less like clubs. This will mean a wholesale reduction. Some parts of government enforce legislation, like consumer affairs and environmental agencies. Others collect data mandated by law, like StatsCan. Still others exist to coordinate national conversations about policy choices. Finance could

Knowledge, Networks and
The Wealth of Nations

Human betterment occurs as we discover cheaper ways to achieve greater results. Knowledge has always been important. The question is, what are the comparative advantages of markets, hierarchies and networks ?

Markets are knowledge machines that reward efficient use of knowledge: that is, the collection of knowledge just to the point at which marginal returns equal marginal costs. Hierarchies reward the over-collection of knowledge, believing that the top "knows" best. Networks, like markets, accumulate knowledge. But they reward the contribution of knowledge to the pool.

For most of human history, knowledge was traditional and more often than not, kept secret by the clans, tribes, guilds and professions that monopolized it. (Some of this still survives, especially in medicine). The result was that the pace of innovation could be controlled by society. But in the west, the complex mix of contending forces interacted through wars, commerce and institutional power struggles (church vs. state, nobility vs. the king, etc.) to break the knowledge monopolies and make innovation relatively sought after. Still, it was a lumpy process that was subject to two major constraints: scarcity of capital and slowness of diffusion. It was hard to raise the money and hard to get new ideas adopted.

The information society, as it succeeds industrial society, operates differently. Knowledge can now be accumulated by anyone at very little cost. Of course, that knowledge is accumulated by people working on different projects and storing that knowledge on hard disks that are accessible through networks. Thousands of commercial data gathering services exist to provide these searchers with the information they require. In addition, electronic forums exist to enable the accumulated knowledge to be discussed and argued over with experts. One of the casualties of this development is the power of information providers who previously had a monopoly on providing information to the powerful: government departments and investment dealers' research organizations. Today, the need for top-heavy departments, advisory councils and other information-processors is open to question. Just as investors have been able to vastly increase their use of financial research because they can do it themselves, the elected officials need smaller and smaller staffs to collect, analyze and process data—or can even do it themselves.

legitimately fit in here, and networking might cure many of its unhelpful fixations on national economic models. These are likely the activities that would survive, and would be enhanced by network structures. As for the others, we'll never miss 'em.

Networks. *Corporations provided the vehicle for mobilizing large amounts of capital used to create the massive industrial infrastructure during the last two decades of the 19th century. Networks facilitate the accumulation and incremental upgrading of massive amounts of knowledge. Just as the vertically integrated trusts of the last century generated efficiency gains that were passed on to the public, networks provide similar economies of scope: a greater variety of tasks for less initial investment can be performed by organizations in networks than those outside them. Networks also reduce the costs of incremental innovation because the installed base can be upgraded rather than replaced.*

Networks are competitive in ways that economists have only just begun to appreciate. Economists used to believe that one network was more "efficient" for its users than two networks covering the same group. Two networks involved doubling the investment to provide essentially the same service, this reasoning went. So networks — at least the capital intensive variety — should be permitted a monopoly, subject to regulation on its rate of return. That's the justification for our much of our hidebound, telecommunications regulation. The problem with that logic is that it assumes technological stability. (Indeed, our telecommunications regulations seek to ENFORCE it!) Competition among companies whether using the same, duplicating or partially linked networks, leads to lower costs and a greater variety of services for the consumer because it imposes tremendous pressure for innovation. How? Each network will compete for the greatest volume of users. True, actual rate of return may be lower and yields less. Paradoxically this will encourage new technologies to try to capture higher yields. Hence the dynamism AND downward pressure on costs.

Years ago, economists sought to define the "optimum size" of networks such that the cost of adding a new member (marginal cost) was equal to the costs of the network divided by its membership (average costs). This worked for water, hydroelectricity and other top-down, non-addressable systems. Today's electronic networks have no copying costs: the cost of adding a new member is always below the average cost. Forcing consumers to choose between networks will raise costs and promote inefficiencies, but allowing consumers to use all networks (promoting compatibility) will promote competition in products and services — in network use.(Your ATM is an addressable system; the phone system is addressable. The water system isn't).The role of network regulation should therefore be the same as regulation elsewhere in the system: prevent monopoly and promote competition.

3

Up & Walking:
The Private Sector

Private sector companies' ability to make policy has gotten vastly better. Always in the lead on globalization, companies have been pushed by ferocious competitive pressures to adjust. They've become far more strategically driven than they were even 15 years ago.

Before the emergence of global markets, when companies were still managed on a country-by-country basis, business would talk strategy, but it was the quarterly result that mattered. Today, companies actually do manage strategically, and short term results are expected to serve the strategic purpose.

Companies and institutional investors alike have been sobered by the fate of those who clung too closely to traditional corporate performance goals to the neglect of strategy: IBM, General Motors and Sears lost their strategic focus. Twenty years ago, they were world wide market leaders: 20 years later, they had vanished from the top 20. Others, who kept or even re-emphasized their strategic focus, like General Electric, Proctor & Gamble, and AT&T, (which went through a massive downsizing in the wake of the court-decreed break-up), have maintained their standing. Still others, like retailing king WalMart and pharmaceutical giant Merck are newcomers, owing to their ability to understand what it is that they do better than anyone else.

Private sector corporations are using the information revolution to improve their ability to manage. The evolution of their networks is enhancing their ability to compete through innovation. Networks involve strategic alliances, joint ventures, cross-licensing and other, less formal agreements for cooperating among companies or even divisions of competing companies. These networks stand, as organizations, part way between the hierarchy of "silo" companies and the market, which is envisaged as operating free of hierarchy and serious imperfection.

Why networks? Because they have two properties companies and markets don't have. One is the increasing benefit to the whole membership from additional individual members. The more members, the more valuable is the network. Plus, the benefits are self-enforcing:

unless you contribute, the other members will stop cooperating with you.

The other property that networks have and companies and markets don't, is they don't have to go step by step. Policy-makers believe research develops in a straight line from pre-competitive research to applied research to product development and test, to launch. But in fact, research is possible anywhere in a networked system and can be captured everywhere in the system if that system is configured to behave that way. Networks have the principle of simultaneous transmission. When one member can see the data, they all can.

Not that corporate information is perfect. Far from it: the state of information about the financial derivatives market for example, is a source of concern to regulators; there's a disturbing lack of transparency on some of the world's biggest equity markets; the conflict of interest implicit in the current corporate auditing system has over the last decade resulted in tremendous losses for investors and a crisis in the accounting profession. And, as with government accounts, there are significant conceptual problems. For example, valuing technological assets, attributing R&D costs and linking pay with performance are areas without clear guidelines.

Nevertheless, companies have moved sufficiently forward that they can live with their data imperfections.

Innovation Benefits From Networks

Consider a problem in which there are 10 possible elements to a solution, each of which bears some relationship to each other. The number of possible solutions, just taking the elements one at a time, is 10 to the 10th power, or 100 billion possible solutions. Clearly, a 10 node network of labs, each one taking 10 possible solutions, could test and communicate the results far faster than could a single, vertical entity. The network permits parallel processing, cooperation and faster results. The benefits can be passed on to consumers or spread throughout the group.

Excuse me?

Compared to most governments, business has adjusted to globalization. It has broken free of national constraints, has found a way to innovate continuously, and make our lives better — leaving aside the question of job loss. Government, over the same time period, has failed to adjust in anything like the same degree. It's been some time since governments have been able to point to real jointly-shared gains arising from public policy. On the contrary, governments have responded to the challenge of the new economy by clinging to outmoded concepts on the one hand and replacing clear vision with short term balancing of stakeholder pressures. Downsizing and deregulation are now occurring, but more as a short-term fix for revenue loss than with a clear strategic goal for the public sector of the future.

The result is that citizens who are not part of a corporate future — and even some who are — find there are no institutions able to articulate an imaginative, yet politically neutral, way forward. It seems like the greatest political hurdle we face is to embrace change and do what we need to do to stay prosperous.

Rogers Cablesystems Ltd., Canada's biggest cable-television company, has struck a deal to test new high-speed, multimedia information transmission technology developed by U.S.-based computer giant International Business Machines Corp.

The companies are indeed talking high-speed. IBM said its so-called PARIS technology can pump out data, voice and video transmissions over fibre-optic links at rates equivalent to transmitting 20,000 single-spaced pages a second.

Rogers officials said that if the IBM technology proves viable and cost-effective, it could give the company's Rogers Network Services division a new service to sell to business telecommunications customers.

One possible application might be for banking, where the technology could be used to transmit complete images of cheques and signatures in very large quantities from one bank or clearing house to another.

From the files of the *ROB*

The 1993 Ford Contour and Mercury Mystique (for the American market) and Ford Mondeo (for the European market) are among the first to be made using a "world car" design. Ford is counting on the consolidation of its North American, European and Asian design operations into a single international network to save millions of dollars and months of work.

A computer network links designers in Dearborn Michigan, Dunton, England; Cologne, Germany; Turin, Italy; Valencia, Calif.; Hiroshima, Japan, and Melbourne, Australia. Here's an example of how it works: a Ford engineer in Dunton dials a few numbers and transmits to Dearborn massive computer files of three-dimensional drawings for a late-nineties sedan. In Michigan, a designer can bring up the drawings on her own workstation, phone her British colleague and work, simultaneously with that colleague, in making on-screen revisions, even rotating the 3-D images to view them from all sides.

A few hours later, the data files might be sent to Ford's design studio in Turin, where a computerized milling machine can turn out a clay or plastic-foam model in a matter of hours. At each of these network stops, Ford is able to take advantage of local expertise or equipment.

The "turnaround" time from conception to production line in the North American industry is 54 months. Ford thinks this new process will cut the lead time to 24 months.

The next step in process technology is "virtual reality" — a computer will recreate the look and feel of a car's interior and send this data through the network so an overseas designer can slip into the virtual driver's seat.

From the files of:
The New York Times Service.

Aided by powerful new technology to send video signals more cheaply either by satellite or private telephone networks, Electronic Data Systems Corp. of Dallas is attempting to breathe new life into the old concept of video conferencing.

The company's Canadian subsidiary, EDS Canada, opened a video conference centre in Ottawa last month to provide what it calls "interactive distance learning."

EDS is a leading designer, operator and integrator of large data-processing and private communication networks.

The company, founded by Texas billionaire H. Ross Perot, was sold to General Motors Corp. in late 1984.

At the heart of EDS's corporate video service is recently developed technology to compress video signals for transmission by satellite.

"Conventional television signals take enormous amounts of capacity on a satellite or phone line to broadcast," Keane Taylor, vice-president of EDS's telecommunications services division, said in an interview. Often, however, companies do not have the network capacity to transmit such a large signal, which is expensive, or a satellite company does not have an entire channel available when a user wants to transmit a video signal.

"The solution is to compress and computerize the signal," Keane said. Once compressed, the television signal needs only a fraction of space on a satellite channel compared with conventional signals. Shrinking a video signal also greatly reduces the cost of broadcasting corporate video productions.

EDS has also developed special computerized touchpads that allow each participant to interact with the instructor at its centre in Ottawa and to electronically "raise a hand" or answer questions on a test.

"We believe corporate training is a key to competitiveness and that interactive video is a cost-effective tool that can make training more affordable for large businesses," said John Bowie, president of EDS Canada.

Citing a study by the Public Service Commission, Mr. Bowie said interactive learning via satellite links can produce savings of more than 60 per cent from the costs of travel.

From the files of the *ROB*

4

New Economy Trashes Old Economics — And Macro Policy Capacity!

From school boards to Rideau Hall, there is a staggering number of politicians in Canada, served by legions of bureaucrats, and still more business managers.

All of these nodes on Canada's power network consult economists for advice. Economists are important beyond their numbers, because powerful people believe what they say about the economy.

Those people may be in business, or in politics or they may be bureaucrats who devise tax, housing, employment, education and other policy. This is problematic for all of us, because if the economists have it wrong, we all get it in the neck and the wallet. And the fact is, most economists have the basic model wrong.

Double Trouble

Actually, economists have two basic models of the economy —a big (macro) economic model that's supposed to tell you how countries and regions work, and a little (micro) economic model that's supposed to tell you how individuals and companies work. Trouble is, macro and micro contradict each other. Micro-economics predicts how companies and individuals will change behaviour in response to changes in the environment. Macro-economics looks at the effects of these big changes — but can't take into account the behaviour changes that will falsify the predictions.

If the way we were taught to look at the economy made for good public policy, the flaws in the model wouldn't matter. From the end of the 1940s to the mid-1970s, the flaws didn't matter all that much. But there's not much good policy around now: it's misfiring because the economy doesn't work the way it used to, or the way the models still say it does.

That's pretty bad. But there's more. If you look at any textbook of micro-economics, you'll see all the diagrams in it are based on smooth, continuous curves. That's so you can use simple math to figure out the relationships.

Trouble is, as economists also learn, companies don't really behave that way. They don't maximize, they optimize: they choose the most possible, not necessarily the best. And optimization is not done smoothly, with nice smooth curves. On the contrary, the way firms change is as lumpy as a discarded mattress.

None of this would matter if it were all just academic brain food. Unhappily, the flaws completely subvert the ability of planners to plan. The flaws mean that the "big picture" economic advice the government receives will be wrong, because as soon as the policy is signalled, people will adjust to undermine it. It also means that the micro-picture policy-makers build up will fail to anticipate change. And it means that the changes individual and companies undertake will happen in bursts that can't be timed or weighed in advance. Result: official predictions will always be wrong (except if they are right by chance), and official explanations will sound airy-fairy. But the mistakes will sap confidence in the future — unless we just agree to ignore them. In which case, the question poses itself, *why pay for them?*

And Still There's More

Economic models are generally based on a more or less Newtonian view of the universe. Newton's view from under the apple tree was that the universe worked with clockwork precision and could be explained by the "forces" of gravity and inertia. In economics, the "forces" of supply and demand, manifested as quantities and prices, interact at points of "equilibrium". This is a radical simplification of what economic historians call "la trame" or "la nappe" — the texture or weave of interactions that make up society.

When it comes to charting the evolution of "la trame" through time, French historians of the so-called Annales school, lead the pack.

Looking at economic change less as a Newtonian phenomenon and more as a social phenomenon in which the weave of social interactions forms the focus of investigation will, ironically, take us back to the earliest and greatest economists who were quick to colour their economic reasoning with a profound knowledge of the way the world actually worked. It is that perspective we must regain if we want to be able to make economic policy and judgements that make any practical sense.

Right away, shifting the focus from theoretical market interactions to the actual effects on human interactions reveals a number of important points:

● economic and social change is continuous only if you take a long view — one of several generations, even centuries, and even then, some choices are made on other-than-strictly-economically rational grounds;

● the shorter perspective shows change to be a series of stop-and-go increases and decreases in output as bottlenecks to change are encountered and overcome.

● what counts in overcoming the bottlenecks is the quality of the social web. In every instance, whether England in the 17th century, France in the 18th century, or the US in the 19th century or Europe in the 20th, just to cite some well-known examples, accommodating modernity involved the tragedy and disruption of civil war and/or revolution. What's more, flaws in one country spilled over to others through the international system.

Thus, the democratization and industrialization of Germany took two world wars (plus two earlier ones restricted to Europe) to accomplish; the shift from industrial society to information society has forced the Soviet Union into receivership and dismantled its eastern Empire. It has also upset the post-war "developed" world's trading and financial systems, trashing trade barriers and floating currencies.

These considerations help explain why Canada's big institutions have been unable to cope with today's modernizing forces: it's like surfing in a hurricane. The question is: in a period of rapid change like our own, what role should public policy play? The answer is: it shouldn't try to slow change down, it should try to facilitate it. Public policy should make the social fabric more absorbent of change. It should work on making the everyday ways we relate to each other — in firms, over the phone, through media and of course through networks— able to accommodate change with fewer lumps and discontinuities. This means taking off the shackles impeding economic activity and developing new policy instruments to help encourage new forms of enterprise.

Our history to date, however, has shown only the most grudging readiness to do this. Instead, in what seems like a preference for the comfort of ritual over the disturbing reality, we cling to the old ways — the old ways of looking at the economy and the old familiar debates — like the constitution, the deficit, the merchandise trade balance, and unemployment, to name but a few.

From Ritual to Reason

Perhaps the most obvious example of how we prefer
ritual to reason in economic debate can be seen in the
way we defer to the categories of the national accounts
and balance of payments tables long after their
appropriateness has been exhausted.

The national accounts are those tables used by
economists to measure economic output. They're the
ones we see when the budget comes out, or when some
organization publishes its forecast. The fundamental
assumptions were developed to explain the world of the
1930s and 40s in which they were invented. Compiling
the accounts means organizing data around a number of
assumptions that seemed self evident half a century ago:

- national economies are identical with national
  boundaries;

- goods and services are two distinctly different outputs;

- ownership and payment are inseparable (i.e. if I owe
  the bank money, my payments will be made to that
  bank);

- capital formation, that is, directly investing in the
  economy, either goes into real estate (land and factory
  buildings) or machinery and equipment;

- inventory gets used up;

- trade and investment are distinctly different.

Hello New Economy

The new economy demolishes each and every one of
those assumptions. An information economy simply

doesn't work the way an national industrial economy works. In a global, information-based economy, economic space is decoupled from national territories, goods and services are indistinguishable.

Take software, for example: is it a good or a service? The difference is only whether an accountant decides to expense it immediately (a service) or depreciate it over time (a good).

Direct investment is another example. Today, direct investment flows into a lot of other things besides the old definitions of capital equipment. For a great many businesses, the mailing lists and other data collected on a hard disk or in a file server are investments. Increasingly, they are the guts of a business: insurance, just-in-time manufacturing, the news business, etc. rely on accumulated data to work.

Take inventory as another example. Information stocks, such as shareware, financial information, market data — anything stored on a bulletin board for download — does not get used up.

Nor can technology investment be depreciated according to some regular schedule. What kills technology investment is the arrival of new technology — substitute technology. Innovation was always important. Think of laundry detergent: it's a huge business, but if a laundry machine manufacturer came up with another way of cleaning clothes that eliminated detergent (ultra sound?), the detergent business would be dead in the wash water, and the commercial value of the old technology would be reduced to zero almost immediately. In today's information economy, competition is based on innovation, and the main barrier to new products is the installed base of the old. IBM's adoption of the DOS operating system made it the world's most widely used computer system. Now, to grow and as well to move into new levels of performance through a better operating system — OS-2 —, IBM has to try to kill DOS off. The success of one is at the expense of the other. Should the "inventories" of both systems be carried as positive on IBM's books and in our national accounts? IBM's situation is typical of all competition based on innovation. Whatever the accountants say, upgrades are additive, and substitutes are a zero-sum contest.

My My, How You've Changed

As for the difference between trade and investment, the information economy blurs this old distinction beyond recognition as well. Imagine a design transferred to a Canadian partner of an Italian firm for the production of a North American version of a product. Should the design be valued at its "import value", say $100,000, or as an Italian asset upon which royalties will be paid over the life of the design and the value of the products into which it is incorporated? Choice number 1 treats the design as a traded article, choice number 2 treats it as a foreign investment.

Finally, the balance of payments debate. Fifty years ago, the world ran on fixed exchange rates. There was no market in products designed to provide coverage against exchange rate fluctuations. In a global economy, however, government policy proved itself too slow and irresponsible to manage exchange rates. Markets overwhelmed any currency bargains fixed at inappropriate levels, as they continue to do. (For example, trashing Europe's managed currency rates in the summer of 1993). Instead, investors turn to products designed to use markets to take the risk out of payments expected in the future. Swaps, hedges, and a variety of other products enable investors who own assets denominated in one currency to be paid in another. They still own the assets, but by swapping the interest streams according to some agreed-upon terms, the investors can insulate themselves from the uncertainties of fluctuating exchange rates. A Japanese investor may therefore buy Canadian bonds but contract with, say, a Canadian investor who owns Yen-denominated instruments, to receive the equivalent Canadian payment in Yen in return for the Canadian receiving the equivalent Yen payment in C$. The point, for our purposes, is that the swap will not show up on the balance of payments: it will still show a picture in which Canadian debt held by foreigners is payable to foreigners — even though the market has re-routed the payment streams back to Canadians.

Putting all these factors together, the conclusion is inescapable. The concepts upon which we base our national accounting are not valid for an information economy. The more our economy evolves in that direction, the worse the errors will become. The economy that works in the old way will have its decline charted with more or less the errors we're used to. The new economic activity will either not be counted or will be wrongly evaluated. Generally speaking, therefore, our economic performance will probably look worse than it really is and our corrective actions will generally be wrong. Certainly, the errors in the system are now greater than the changes the system claims to measure.

Is It Fish or is It Fowl?

What is left of the distinctions among the four basic economic operations of consuming, saving, investing and trading (importing and/or exporting)? In most cases, we can no longer reliably tell the difference. For example, if you expense your new software in the year you buy it, then the national economic statisticians call it a consumption item. Yet the software resides on your hard disk, continuing to perform, clearly not "consumed" in the usual meaning of the term. Only if you depreciate it over time is it treated as an investment. But the useful life of software is unpredictable —it's useful until a better program comes along.

Another problem is the definition of manufacturing. If you are employed by a "manufacturing" company, what you do is manufacturing, even if it is really market research or design. But if you did the same job outside the company, as a consultant to it, then it would be classified as a service, and not manufacturing. Among other things, this means that our count of "production workers" upon which much of our productivity conclusions are based is conceptually incorrect. When those numbers refer to assembly line workers, they may be perfectly accurate. But increasingly, manufacturing involves service activities.

Investment or trade? If you export or import a design template which is subsequently used in millions of products, was that template an import or an investment? The answer depends whether you paid a fixed charge or a royalty. These are just "one more thing" to face up to. Our definitions of economic statistical categories reflect the 1930s and 40s when they were developed; they do not reflect the interdependent, information-based economy of the 1990s.

This litany of flaws is by no means exhaustive. These are simply the clearest. The upshot: because our scorekeeping is wrong, the policy capacity of government to adjust to the information economy is severely flawed. As long as we debate the adjustment issues following the national accounts, there will be little factual basis for conclusion. Because of the confusions mentioned above, we don't know the merchandise trade balance or the services trade balance. We don't know how much foreign investment we have, we don't know how much capital accumulation is going on. When we say the economy's growing at 1.5 per cent or even 3.4 per cent, we really have no basis for those assertions. Even at the level of specific industries, there's no agreed upon accounting treatment for software, traded designs or research undertaken conjointly in a network. Technological obsolescence is nowhere a factor. Nor, for that matter, are environmental considerations. True, something is being recorded. But the picture is so partial and the elements so confused that they no longer provide an adequate basis for policy advice. The inescapable conclusion is that the global information economy effectively undermines existing government policy capacity, especially at the level of macro economic policy. Continuing to dwell on them will ignore the important changes going on in the micro-economy and instead lock us into old policy alternatives.

Are there any new directions? Perhaps just because the focus is global, the new directions and new instruments appropriate to government policy in the information age are beginning to evolve in trade policy. In order to see why, it is instructive to step back a bit and consider

briefly how technology—specifically the atomic bomb—
changed the meaning of national defence. We shall then
see that with the end of the cold war some of these
changes are spilling over into trade.

Learning to Love the Bomb

Einstein said that the nation state and the split atom
couldn't coexist. The cold war is now over. And after
1945, the atomic bomb was never used. Does that mean
Einstein was wrong? This a complex subject. But the
essence of it is that the atomic bomb was never used
because countries developed a practice of deterrence,
based on the idea of mutual destruction. At the heart of
the deterrence doctrine was a terrible paradox: the best
national defence was to offer your population as a
hostage to the other power. The best national defence in
the atomic age became in effect the abandonment of pre-
atomic age national defence.

Throughout the cold war, technological competition
continued to assure that this mortal contract was
maintained. Perhaps the most persuasive case against Star
Wars — the proposed US defence against a strategic
missile strike — was that it upset this terrible balance.
Those who lived through this period — namely most
people now living — grew so accustomed to being
hostages to one superpower or another that we accepted
it as a defence policy. Yet historically it was the complete
opposite of what defence policy used to be about. The
best example of a classic defence policy before the cold
war is England's policy between the Napoleonic war and
the two German wars: the walls of oak, the blue water
naval policy. There was no mortal paradox here: the role
of British defence forces was to preserve the Empire
from harm — not offer it up in a deadly exchange.

Deterrence and Trade: "Strategic" Trade Theory

As nuclear technology turned defence policy on its head, so globalization and information technology has turned economic policy on its head. You can see this obviously in current discussions of trade policy. Trade policy used to be based rather unquestioningly on the belief that free trade made the pie bigger by promoting international specialization. The more open the trading regime, the more each country would concentrate its economic activities in those fields in which it was relatively good. If all countries did that, obviously world output would grow faster, productivity would rise and input costs would fall. Some would still be better off than others, but all would be better off than before.

Since the cold war's end, many trade specialists have been looking at those traditional arguments more closely. The old explanations assumed the world was composed of national companies who traded at a distance from each other. The new explanation assumes that the world is a complicated place in which investment is a precursor to trade and that large multinational companies do most of the investment. International trade is, moreover, crucial to the success of those investments and national barriers that distort investment decisions will also distort trade. What kind of rules will adequately protect national interests with respect to multinational investment that at the same time won't discourage investment from occurring?

Gradually, an answer is emerging among economists that qualifies their earlier endorsement of free trade—a belief that "composition" matters, in other words, a view that some sectors are likely to promote national welfare more than other sectors, and that national trade policy should serve the needs of those sectors.

The new answer to ensuring open flows of "strategic" investment is so-called "strategic" trade theory. Those who argue for such "strategic" trade policies are paradoxically arguing the state should use trade barriers to open foreign markets—a set of arguments that is actually a branch of nuclear age defence theory.

The arguments go like this: For a big project that needs lots of money and promises lots of spillover benefits along with it — like a new generation supersonic airliner — it makes sense for governments to add their strength to those of their national companies to deter other potential suppliers out of the game. If they succeed — or even reduce the number of potential suppliers — they will increase the returns to their national investment. By announcing they—the government— will subsidise companies to produce below cost, they will chill the efforts of foreign rivals who don't have similar government support. By this limiting of the number of potential rivals, they will gain monopoly or quasi-monopoly returns and pay back the subsidies more quickly.

This line of reasoning suggests that the role of government in a high-tech, capital intensive world is to intervene on behalf of national champions. The policy question facing government in a global economy, therefore, is often taken to be, how to choose the champions to back. However, this is only part of the story—the least significant part. The real question, as with all threats, is how to make the threat credible. Clearly, being known to have deep pockets and for the ardent support of national champions already is one such way. Also, the stakes involved must be proprotionate to the threat. This in turn reduces the number of alternative target industries.

Carrying the argument one step further, however, poses the question, what if every government succeeded in creating credible national champions in the industries they thought most important to them? The result would clearly be a global price war in flagship projects that ensures no nation would ever recoup its initial investment. International poverty and a slowdown in the pace of innovation, not greater prosperity, would result from everyone playing that game. Even more important for a country like Canada, whose relatively shallow pockets are nevertheless deep in the red, the strategic competition formula is a formula for moving important technology to bigger, richer, countries.

Taking strategic trade theory seriously, therefore, leads to the same conclusions as deterrence theory: that open trading and investment systems are best but can be enhanced only by threatening to destroy them.

Such in fact has been U.S. economic policy during the Bush and Reagan periods. Recently the deterrence aspects have clearly been screwed up several notches. (For example, the Chief Economic Advisor, Ms. Laura D'Andrea Tyson believes that there should be reciprocity agreements on R&D between countries, effectively cartelizing research in so-called "strategic" sectors. And DARPA, the Defense Advanced Research Projects Agency, is refusing to permit U.S.-based affiliates of foreign-owned companies to participate in its pre-competitive research consortia. Previous U.S. administrations had won the right of U.S. company affiliates to participate in European pre-competitive projects). But in today's trading world, the temptation to cheat on multi-lateral rules-based trading arrangements is such that many trade experts believe that only credible deterrence can forestall it. So, as in defence, the global trading state preserves the world trading order by threatening to wreck it: behind every successful agreement lies a high stakes game of subsidy chicken.

Where Does This Logic Leave A Small Country Like Canada?

The parallel between defence policy and economic policy in this line of reasoning is obvious. Only big economic powers can engage in the kind of mutual deterrence that will produce trade gains. Smaller powers, therefore, have a special problem. Small countries should pick their allies so as to be included in this game and, at the same time, keep multilateral institutions alive because that is ultimately where most disputes will be resolved. Similarly, the more smaller powers a large player can gather under its umbrella is also threat enhancing.

Viewed from this perspective, the FTA and NAFTA are clearly useful policies for Canada to pursue. They bring us into sizeable trading blocs that can press for more open global trading arrangements. (Of course, questions arise when the major partner actually becomes more protectionist, as it did when major nuclear powers passed through periods of enhanced bellicosity.)

What of multilateralism, that is, the reenergizing of rules-based trade resting on the gentlemanly undertaking of the GATT (General Agreement on Tariffs and Trade, the principal framework for international trade)? A beguiling but increasingly hopeless prospect. Clearly, the emergence of strong regional blocs permits those blocs to rely less on on-going negotiation and more on threats of attack and reprisal to maintain and enlarge open trading and investment relations. There is every indication this is proving to be more effective than relying on institutions like GATT– or, more precisely, that trade deterrence (or lack of it) is what is bedevilling the closing stages of the Uruguay Round of GATT negotiations.

It is not in the interests of smaller powers to see the effectiveness of multilateral institutions decline. Otherwise, world trade and investment rules will be made exclusively by the big economies. But this pessimistic alternative overlooks the role of global enterprise as the real constraint on even big countries' ability to achieve anything unilaterally. From a company perspective, the regional arrangements necessary for big countries to increase their "deterrent" power create opportunities for small countries to become marginally more "investment-friendly" than the large countries — wherein lies their real bargaining strength. Canada, for instance, has exceptional access to US markets. But it has a better social system so that, other things being equal, Japanese and European investors wanting to enter or expand in North America without incurring the public safety problems of life in the US might consider Canada. (However, there are also special reasons why other considerations, including non-tariff barriers the negotiations failed to remove, might cause that investment to remain targeted at the US.)

The upshot of this? Many of us still talk as though we believe governments have the capacity to shield us from global economic developments. But in fact governments no longer have that capacity. The mobility of capital and production means that no policy change that leaves someone even relatively worse off can be enforced. Instead, the "victims" will shift resources to where they can't be taxed. If all loopholes are closed, then the money won't come at all. Nor can general trade or capital barriers be imposed without reducing benefits overall. These changes drastically reduce the ability of governments to make useful policy based on redistribution.

Yet interestingly, even small governments are not completely helpless. For one thing, Canada's attractive power for international direct investment is enhanced by attempting to reduce the anomalies inherent in free trade based on national treatment.

National treatment means that international companies are treated like domestic ones. This makes sense in integrated trading areas like North America. Trouble is, companies that integrate across borders are subject to trade law; their strictly domestic competition is not.

Subsidies for instance. Unlike the past, today's production is carried on by integrated, interdependent processes in each region. Transborder enterprises involved in networks share designs, parts, and production facilities to create parts of the final product which they exchange so that each network node can assemble the final product while concentrating on producing one or two of its vital components. Production capacity in these enterprises is managed at least regionally and often globally.

Subsidies can affect location decisions of those enterprises. But without trade barriers, it makes little economic sense to permit some regions to produce at less cost than other regions because the goods will trade freely and what you gain in one region, you'll lose in another.

By the same logic, it makes even less economic sense to outlaw subsidies between countries in the same region yet allow subsidies between sub-national regions within countries to distort market forces. Yet that is current trade law allows.

Guaranteeing national treatment to foreign companies —the underlying basis of the FTA and NAFTA as well as GATT — ensures that each country applies its own rules in its own territory with no discrimination against the foreign company. So now Californian subsidies to firms that compete with Canadian firms for sales to, say Louisiana, are perfectly legal. Yet Canadian products subsidized from Ontario are subject to trade problems.

But the deal is not perfect. For one thing, there is a major failure in the FTA that was not present in our Canada-U.S. defence arrangements. It is that the FTA and the NAFTA, fully consistent with GATT, failed either to limit government support of strategic technology at the critical initial stages or to guarantee access to government-funded pre-competitive research on a national treatment basis. This in effect multiplies the attractive powers of big countries at the expense of smaller.

Such opportunities existed under the Defence Procurement arrangements used for NORAD. Perhaps some Exxon-Florio rules of our own — the rules that the US uses to limit so-called foreign participation in R&D on national security grounds — would help Canadians gain better access to US projects.

Consumer law is another area needing attention. When cross border shopping can be done by television or computer modem (modems are gizmos that let computers talk to each other) and credit cards, it makes little sense that consumer laws on each side of the border are unable to enforce the warranties from the other country.

Despite these and other issues, the FTA has achieved most of the things its supporters expected. Higher exports to the US, more or less effective dispute panels to more or less de-politicize trade rulings, etc.

The challenge for Canada and Canadian-based suppliers is to participate in innovation without being forced into an unsustainable position — either through excessive development costs or through followership that generates few benefits.

Conclusion: New Ways for Old

This chapter has argued that the nation state has in effect lost it as far as making nationally-based policies are concerned. The statistical concepts are outmoded, the ability to protect national space depends on the deterrent power of regional blocs, and traditional policy instruments— such as subsidies, fines, taxes — can have their painful aspects avoided by international corporate networks.

Yet the same conditions do allow governments to achieve policy goals by other means. These means are the means used by networks—connect (or disconnect), store and forward.

Take the subsidy issue yet again. Canada's position in the situation outlined above—no subsidies within or across borders—would be supported by the competitors of the California firm. If they knew about it. The Canadian government can help them find out just by publishing the address of a bulletin board that contains an inventory of US subsidies at the state level. Such research is ongoing at the US Policy Studies Group, Dalhousie University, and its principal researchers have an Internet address. Policy instrument: connect, and perhaps support the researcher's ability to store and forward his findings. Similarly, forwarding and posting information about Canada's internal trade barriers will lead to increased pressure to reduce them.

Take the issue of accessing pre-competitive research. Establishing a similar program in Canada in areas of Canadian excellence, then shared on a network basis with others. The instruments: connect, store, forward, and post for network members.

Canada already has the connections in place to do this: Canole—the network linking Canadian research libraries—and Bitnet, the academic branch of Internet. Plus hundreds of bulletin boards all over the country, including Canada Remote Systems, the bulletin Board voted best by readers of *Boardwatch*, the most authoritative magazine on BBSing.

5

Overcoming Change Fatigue Syndrome

When Fernand Braudel, one of the world's great economic historians, sat down to write the first of three volumes in his history of the global economy *(A History of Material Life, 3 vols., Harper & Row, 1979)*, his first thought was to call volume one, "The Possible and the Impossible: Mankind Faces Everyday Life."

He later changed it to "The Structures of Everyday Life".

It turns out that when it comes to discussing economic change, the standard economists' abstractions — savings, investment, consumption and trade — are no longer enough. To really understand and describe what happens in an economy, you have to think of it in terms of what every new day presents to people.

Economics as economists do it identifies component parts of the economy and oversimplifies their inter-relationship so that behaviour can be discussed. But the categories used to describe the operations of the market are insufficient to give us a complete description of material life. As Braudel's magnificent books show, an economy encompasses not only market activity, but also the limits to market activity — the daily interactions of everyday life that are governed by habit and the uses of things, in addition to calculations of gain and loss that drive market activity. In charting the evolution of mankind's fluctuating prosperity, the movements of that dividing line between what the market covers and the other possibilities life offers plays a major determining role. When we try to evaluate Canada's present condition and prospects, it is the placement of that dividing line that we now have to face up to.

Life in the Fast Lane

From the 1970s onward — from the first and second oil crises in particular — Canada has experienced enormous changes that have profoundly affected our economy as well as the fabric of everyday life. At the global level, we've packed a lot into 20 years.

We have also seen the development of a global economy,

The future of resource-based development
(circa 1975)

In the late 1970s, it was a prevailing view among Canadian decision-makers that natural resource prices, especially oil and gas, would continue to rise relative to the prices of manufactured goods, thus reversing a historic relationship and paving the way for a new economic order dominated by commodity producers. Our effort to implement this strategy was the National Energy Program. As everyone now knows, prices soon went into reverse as the market adjusted to new conditions. But the misallocated investment remained a huge opportunity cost that kept Canadian productivity growth flat for the rest of the decade — plus, constitutionally poisoning relations between the centre and the regions of the country, the legacy of which "haunts us still".

The full impact of Japanese manufacturing competition.

Herman Kahn first alerted North America to the new Japanese industrial strengths in the mid-1960s, and many observers tried to warn North American car makers about an emerging shift in consumer patterns towards smaller cars. Nobody paid attention (what's new?). Both developments got an extra kick from the oil crisis. Result: By the mid 1980s, the Japanese had captured virtually all of the small car market, their consumer electronics companies had driven virtually every North American manufacturer into other businesses, and managers were scrambling around trying to learn the "secrets of Japanese management". Within a short time, US companies were automating assembly lines and otherwise investing massively in technology. But heavy investment in new process technology was only part of the story. The other part involved the sociology of the work place: people and how they deal with each other. That was the part we didn't want to hear about. So we only got half the results we expected.

the collapse of communism, and the emergence into the world marketplace of about 300 million inhabitants of the former Soviet Union and its eastern European empire.

We've seen the successful economic development of the Asian dragons — South Korea, Taiwan, Hong Kong, Singapore and Malaysia — from low income countries to middle income countries whose cost structures are about the same as those of Mexico; they are now uncompetitive with the real low wage countries like Sri Lanka. We are also beginning to experience the impact of new, double digit growth rates in China and India.

The response to those developments has helped change North America from a capital exporting region to a capital importing one: this region used to take in so much money in payment for exports that it had billions to lend or invest in other parts of the world. Canada still exports more merchandise than it imports, but the surplus is shrinking. Both Canada and the United States borrow capital from other parts of the world to finance their spending. The response to 20 years of extraordinary change has helped transform the way we think about world trade, to cause two major GATT rounds — Tokyo and (maybe) Uruguay — to liberalize world trade in the light of the stunning exporting successes, first of the Japanese, later of the other Asian powers. At the same time, we have also seen the universal trading system modified by the emergence of three regional blocs, or triads: North America, the European Community and the looser Asia-Pacific regions. More trade and investment goes on within each regional bloc than between regions. Nevertheless, global trade and investment between regions continues to outstrip any country's domestic economic growth.

These global changes have altered the geo-political map. Behind them lie many factors, but the factor most instrumental in bringing them about has been extraordinary technological change in information and telecommunications technologies. Computers have shrunk from room-sized to desk-top to lap-top to notebooks. (You don't need a keyboard anymore if your handwriting's clear). These machines can talk to each other. Desktop computers hooked up over phone lines have changed the world — first by revolutionizing capital markets, second, by revolutionizing goods production and the provision of services. These are some of the "process" technologies that displace factory workers and middle managers. They have also changed business in amazing ways: in just a decade, big publicly traded firms have gotten bigger. Most global manufacturing is done by firms in the $8 billion to $80 billion revenue range. Big firms have shed their side businesses and focused on the "core", seeking to maximize value of the core through alliances with other mega-companies to gain access to the world's biggest markets. The sum of all these changes means we no longer produce goods the way we used to and we no longer provide services the way we used to.

No wonder so many of us seem to suffer from chronic change fatigue syndrome. In a generation, we've moved from mass production to just-in-time, flexible manufacturing to today's mass customizing "agile" manufacturing systems. Just over the horizon: the so-called virtual corporation, if we can work out the legal wrinkles in time. (How do we enforce obligations on a company that exists for a few weeks or a few months?)

Something Going On

Our organization of work has moved from Taylorism with its routinized, mass workforce doing repetitive, boring jobs, to today's cross-trained, empowered workforce, accepting responsibility for output quality, analyzing problems and implementing solutions.

Services, too, have undergone dramatic changes. Fast-food chains like McDonald's, Burger King, and Pizza Pizza, whatever you think of the diet, represent a similar application of process technology to the restaurant business. The giant warehouse stores like Price Club and Costco use computerized process technology to lower the cost of service and pass on the savings to consumers. That's had devastating consequences to department stores. Catalogue shopping and home shopping over television are also examples of new process technology changing industry structure.

Many people associate the disruptions we're experiencing with free trade. But it's not trade agreements that are making the difference, it's new and different ways of working. Free trade is a requirement, because today's process technology can co-ordinate efficient production across continents. Trying to protect ourselves with trade barriers simply impedes the functionality of these new systems and reduces the incentives to invest in them, with all the negatives that go with an uncompetitive production base. Free trade and trade agreements are a follow-on — a ratification of an already existing reality.

Nevertheless, the new process technology destabilizes the way the country's regions relate to each other and to Ottawa. The new technology obliges firms to source world wide with tightly scheduled just-in-time delivery. In Canada, that means mainly north - south trade, with continental production arranged to link regions in the US and Canada. Provinces now trade as much or more with the US than with each other. This throws the transfer payments of the federal system into disarray: if Ontario's best customers are in the US, not western Canada, why should Ontario add to its costs (and risk losing those customers) to send money to other provinces? It was different when equalization payments were a kind of good customer rebate. Now they're more like having an alcoholic in the family whose consumption patterns are blowing holes in the budget and threatening the family firm with bankruptcy.

What About Unemployment?

Where have all the jobs gone in this brave new world of process technology? Again, it's not the technology that's cost the jobs. On the contrary, our adaptation to this technology has preserved the jobs we have. The jobs are lost because of the interaction of this new technology and the way firms compete with each other. If managers had foreseen the applications of the new technologies, they could have taken the lead in reconfiguring their businesses. Had they done that, they would have made money that would flow back into the economy, creating

Take steel. Cold rolled steel is a mass produced product, a triumph of industrial technology that makes high quality steel available for general purpose use—especially pipelines, automobiles and construction. Its triumph is its ability to transform iron ore into high quality steel at an exceptionally good price per ton.

Trouble is, the mass market served by cold rolled steel can be segmented into some specialty markets that can be served with a lesser quality steel if it comes at a lower price. Especially smaller cars and other low margin products made for market niches. Steel for these markets can be adequately produced by so-called minimills. The people who realized this transformed the industry. And they weren't Canadian. Canadians were late to leave mass produced cold-rolled steel and late into minimills. The people who were ready for change first transformed scrap into steel that was good enough for many applications and was cheaper. Competitive pressure obliged the steel users to switch. To compete, our mass producer had to become a specialty producer—now specializing in high quality, cold-rolled steel. Result: job loss in the high capacity producer.

work opportunities for people who were downsized out of their industry. But for the last decade or more, most Canadian companies weren't making profits, and a lot of whatever money was made was misapplied to unproductive takeovers.

That's what structural unemployment is all about. It's not a technology issue, it's a strategy issue. Timing is everything, in life and in business, as in love. (However, the flip side, re-employing the displaced worker is a technology issue, because without the technology, the re-employment strategy won't work.)

All these economic changes have been accompanied by a raft of social ones: the changing family, more opportunity for women in the workplace, especially as owner-operators of small businesses, the breakdown of consensus on the role of schools, the drop in real incomes, the demands for government to do more, to do less and to do more with less, and more besides. A generation ago, most families were like the "Leave It to Beaver", "Father Knows Best" model. Now only a minority are. A generation ago, official school drop out rates were lower, but fewer children saw a university-bound future for themselves and there were more opportunities for people who lacked a full 12 years of schooling. A generation ago, wealth seemed to be based on economic resources and governments seemed to have control over their economic space. There was also a demographic curve bringing unprecedented numbers of people into the big consumption years — marriage, house, kids, school, etc. The possibilities seemed open, and if the vision was of a life marginally less consumer-oriented than Dad's, attainment nevertheless seemed assured.

Now in addition to the impact of Asian competition and billions of dollars of new investment in process technology, we also need to acknowledge that society has changed in other ways, too. More boomers' marriages ended in divorce with single parent families; the hoped-for resource-based future failed to materialize; and now the bill is coming due for the short-term government fixes; plus, the kids are now ready for university, without which their future would be even grimmer. The possibilities seem as open — maybe even more open — than before. But the list is very different: entrepreneurship and global competition, rather than a cushy corporate or public sector job-for-life; solid technology training as a basis for life rather than the arts and humanities, even economics; and a Canada organized on very different lines. As for families? A generation ago, Mom cooked dinner and the kids sat down to eat. Now everyone throws something into the microwave when they get a chance.

Along with the boundaries of material life, the boundaries of political and emotional life have changed as well. Today's structures of everyday life are certainly linked with the past because we've all been there. But that was then. This is now.

A Political Culture of Refusal

Clearly, we've been through a lot. Yet even though we're prepared to admit it to ourselves and in conversation with our friends, these changes in everyday life are not reflected in our public life or our public policies. About half the voters in the last election (October 25, 1993) were prepared to vote for Reform or the Bloc Quebecois, and these parties were more prepared than the others to cast aside a lot of veils — the Bloc on confederation, the Reformers on the role of government. But the Liberals got the most votes and their appeal was the most nostalgic of all. The more obvious the changes, the more desperately a plurality among us seem to cling to our images of the past. Canada has developed a political culture of refusal to take the present on its own terms and deal with it.

Total Quality Management: grinding to a halt. The main successes have been with the subsidiaries of US firms who are obliged to adopt international quality practices as a condition of remaining within the company network. Many of these companies have also been able to bring along their key Canadian suppliers. Some large Canadian companies, too, especially some of the banks, are endeavouring, with mixed results, to implement quality programs.

But beyond the charmed circle of the top 100 companies or so that account for most of our exports, especially our end product exports, quality programs are failing. Among the reasons identified are that many small manufacturers are unable to install the process control technology necessary to qualify for ISO 9000, the internationally recognized quality standard. Another reason, more fundamental, is that many factory owner-operators do not wish to grant their work force the necessary power over the job. This will persist until our small manufacturer base is reorganized into a more sophisticated, interactive networked manufacturing base.

Don't hold your breath for this to happen. What we are really seeing is an attempt by Canadians — as we saw in the election to some extent — to avoid changing the social fabric any more.

We seem to be reaching the limits to change here. The culture of refusal to confront and accept the world as it is, the suspicion of new approaches, — all these things are putting change on hold for now. Increasingly, Canada is deciding to wait — to wait for the deficit and the debt to return to manageable proportions, to wait for an economic recovery, to wait for the development of an "information highway", to wait for the advent of something different, rather than pressing on with change.

As a justification for this cultural refusal, we are also witnessing the creation of a number of myths. One is that productivity kills jobs. Another is that technology kills jobs. Now we know from more than 200 years of economic experience that both statements are false. If they were true, the US and Japan would have the world's highest unemployment because they are the most productive and because they use the most advanced technology. In fact, they have the world's lowest unemployment rates.

The myth can't even be supported by Canadian numbers. Canada is the world's second most productive economy, overall. But our manufacturing sector is somewhere in the middle of the G-7 pack. So our productivity edge has to come from — where? That's right — services, which also happens to be where the most jobs are. Yet like the urban legends about crocodiles in the New York sewers, the myths of job-slaying products and technology persist. Trouble is, sometimes policy-makers believe them.

You might wonder, as both of us do, why Canadian leaders are not doing more to explain the changes the country has been through and help encourage the country through the changes it needs to make. Instead, as the election showed, they prefer to try to bamboozle us with the old time snake oil of quick fixes — of PAUSES, A HALT To, etc. — instead of helping us understand the nature of the changes we've been going through and what we have to do next.

For we cannot just put Canada on hold until some people catch their breath. The pain, the unemployment, the slow growth, even the deficits and debt, are not coming from too much change. On the contrary, they are the product of too LITTLE change. The price of stopping change is the price we see being paid all around us: the million and a haalf unemployed, mostly 15-24 year-olds with less than 12 years schooling, the decline of the cities (which we unaccountably restrict to a property tax base), the pressure on social programs that impede change instead of promote it, the pressure on confederation.

As we argue in the sections that follow, a determined effort to cast off the self-imposed restraints on the way we do things— especially in financial services, telecommunications and education—would go a very long way to turning our current decline around. To get there, though, we have to overcome our unwillingness to confront the new world on its own, new terms. We have to do things differently. If we want to change direction, we have to change course.

6

October 26, 1993 Canada: The Morning After

Canada, the morning after the election, got a legislature in which all the country's fault lines are exposed, and a majority Liberal government in which both sides of the economic policy debates of the last 10 years are represented but hardly resolved.

Despite the criticisms of first-past-the-post voting systems, the result is remarkable in its combination of power, pessimism and economic differences.

Reform and the Bloc Quebecois both advocate policies based on the proposition that Canada as is can't work. Their presence is a major defeat not just for the old line parties as campaigners, but also for the delicate balancing mechanisms of their caucuses. The constituent political parts of Canada — having proven incapable of resolving their differences in private ways the electorate would support — must now air them daily. The political rips are now clearly revealed: will confronting them publicly help heal them? The answer is not clear — the first test will be the Quebec provincial election in 1994.

Somewhat ironically, the election also changes the economic polarities of Canadian politics. Previously, our economic rifts were debated openly (is credit too easy or too tight, should government stimulate or discourage spending? Is there enough money being distributed to the poor, the regions, the unemployed? Are taxes too high or too low?), and our political rifts resolved behind closed doors (regional distribution of government projects, constitutional positions such as who should have what power, etc.) Now this has reversed. Virtually every opposition seat (except for the nine NDP members) is occupied by someone elected on a platform of deficit reduction. The majority government remains internally divided on economic policy, between traditional expansionists and advocates of restraint, between supporters of free trade and advocates of trade accord renegotiation — divisions that used to dominate public debate but which will now (maybe) be resolved in caucus while the political row goes on in public.

Lots of ink and newsprint will be used up explaining and interpreting this outcome. But a single clear test is now starkly confronting us: can Canada generate joint gains, gains we all participate in, gains that will make people happier about keeping Canada going as a single national account?

If Canada cannot find a way to generate joint gains, in which we all want to share, then the country will fragment into its regional parts. And as taxpayers, we will be paying our political elites to squabble over "just" shares of the national assets. Again, there is a simple economic test about whether this outcome is a good one. Will these national assets — the elements of wealth in the 21st century — be gaining or losing value at that point? If Canada really is as broken as many of its critics think it is, then the official break up of the country should lead to higher asset values. The break-up should generate the gains that keeping the country going chews up.

We may be closer to that point than we think. British Columbia and Alberta have Canada's most robust economies. They, together with Ontario — the biggest casualty of the recession in terms of job loss — are required to pay equalization payments to Atlantic Canada, via Ottawa. If they weren't obligated to make those payments, they could cut taxes, grow faster, and pay down their own debt more quickly. If they didn't have to send the money through Ottawa's bureaucracy, they could send less to the rest of the country for the same effect.

Quebec is basically on the cusp: unlike the provinces to the west of it, the rest of Canada is its best customer. The rest of Canada is also its best source of incoming funds. But Quebec taxpayers also contribute a roughly equal amount to Ottawa. True, some is returned in the form of federal contracts and investments. But Quebecers argue they would rather spend the money on their own priorities, not those of another government. Federalists argue that Quebec has increased fiscal room to pursue its own objectives because it can opt out of federal programs and redirect the money, and also because of the creation of the Caisse de Dépôt et Placements which receives the pension money of all Quebeckers' and invests according to "Quebec-first" priorities. While the facts provide evidence that Quebeckers investment decisions have failed to show better than average returns, Quebeckers say, "So What!" It feels better to raise and spend your own money, rather than have someone else do it for you.

Underlying these considerations is the real worm in the apple: Ottawa's growing debt. The federal debt is now equivalent to about half the value of the goods and services Canada produces in a year, and like the product of a demented battery maker, it just keeps on growing and growing. Bringing Canada to an end — at least as we know it today — would have the single virtue of ending central government borrowing. That selling point alone could be enough to bring Canada to an end, especially if handling the debt service means severe cuts in living standards.

These are very serious pressures on any political arrangement. Such serious problems in the treasury go a long way toward explaining many of the sea changes we find throughout history. The spread of Islam across North Africa as far as Spain more than 1,000 years ago; the collapse of feudalism four hundred years ago; Britain's loss of the 13 colonies; the origins of the French

Revolution two hundred years ago, to name but a few. Whether the British North America Act can resist forces of this magnitude is unclear: readers will have their own estimates of the probabilities.

The international reaction to selling off the assets of the country and divvying them up are as predictable as anything is. Capital markets would go nuts for a while because international investors wrongly believe Ottawa, in the final analysis, stands behind provincial debt. Just as corporations try to do when they break up or wind down, much of the volatility could be exorcised by thinking through the necessary financial needs. One can imagine a special bond issue designed to help the country pay down its combined debts as part of the wind-up deal. Since it would include no new central government borrowing, that would amount to a substantial benefit for the shareholders.

Arithmetically, in other words, the economic case for the viability of Canada is growing weaker every day the current fiscal regime persists. The fact that the newly elected Liberal government was elected on a platform based on traditional, time worn clichés about government (I have the plan, I have the people; $6 billion infrastructure program, I will replace the GST...) suggests it will be some time before they attack this problem. Will they find a solution before one is imposed on them? Again, readers will come to their own conclusions.

Beyond the fiscal arithmetic, however, lies the symbolic effect of Canada's collapse. For many people, Canada represents one of the world's last big ideas: a vast, peaceful northern land that against the odds has become a symbol of hope that a handful of people who are quite different in many ways can still achieve great things together. The enormous geographic scale and climatic harshness is the point. Judging from the composition of the current parliament — two opposition parties of equal size, each representing the views of people who have long felt alienated from the federal decision-makers and each region resentful of the other — maybe the Canadian idea's not so compelling anymore. Certainly, it will be more difficult than ever to sustain.

The Bind that Ties

This is the bind we're in right now. Cutting government and deficits is critical if we're going to get a government we can afford. But shrinking government as an economic actor could also undermine what fragile confidence there is left in the economy. More and more consumers will leave their short term deposits in the bank instead of using them to go on buying sprees. Domestic demand will stay stuck to the floor. But the alternative policy—new public spending or looser monetary policy— would only pile up debt and weaken the economy more.

After nine years of allegedly conservative government in Ottawa in which policies were designed, but failed, to reduce the deficit; in which policies were designed, but failed, to find some new constitutional deal, perhaps we should look elsewhere for solutions to Canada's problems, especially its economic difficulties. As argued in earlier chapters, the big picture, the macro-picture, cannot provide its own solutions. Why? Principally because the rules of the economic game have changed. The solutions will be found by looking at the micro-world of everyday life and the transformations that are — or are not — taking place there.

In the chapters that follow, we will examine some industries and identify some relatively simple changes that could trigger a new dynamism in the Canadian economy. Only by unleashing the latent potential in this country will we create the joint gains that will heal our divisions and get on top of our fiscal problems before they bury us.

7

Defusing The Crisis of Representation

"Policy should bubble up from below. The success of British institutions is founded on evolution, not revolution..." These and other shibboleths are at the root of Canada's system of government at the federal and provincial levels. And, as everyone knows, these institutions are in trouble.

Parliament, supposedly elected to represent the voters to the government, mostly represents the government to the voters with some limited exceptions in caucus. Government, through its system of whips and patronage, has transformed the parliamentary process into a temporary dictatorship, in which opinion polls, not parliament, is the major check on bad or unpopular policy.

L ike Woody Allen's satiric view of film-making, some legislation starts as an idea, moves on to a concept, and only after public opinion is prepared will the concept become a bill for parliament's consideration. Other legislation begins as a consultation project among bureaucrats and prominent stakeholder groups. As the government's goals become clearer, it may become an occasion for stakeholder lobbying "at the political level" among ministers. Only after this process has thoroughly massaged the package will it be introduced to parliament. Like a menu at a Chinese restaurant, there are many combinations to use to orchestrate public debate before bills get to parliament.

Governments typically try to dominate this pre-legislative phase and use it to scope out the contours of public opinion. This phase in effect bypasses parliament, although caucus may be briefed on progress depending on the issue. Opinion polls test public reaction to possible alternatives, in effect substituting for elected representatives.

Once in parliament, the government can get its way, but tradition usually constrains it to take technical amendments after parliament approves the legislation in principle. Consequently, the committee stage following second reading is very often an occasion for major improvements. Parliamentarians generally earn their money at this stage but, typically, only those with a particular interest in the bill pay much attention to this process. Specialized reporting agencies cover this process in detail and Canadian Press usually has someone watching for news. Committees are often covered on the parliamentary cable TV channel. But getting these technical, boring discussions into prime time is virtually impossible. So most people never see what is very often a constructive process.

The bureaucracy, which used to have a virtual monopoly on policy development, is now effectively balanced by interest groups which can use the media and political consultants to good effect at the political level. Failure to do a good job on preparation can result in the bill being publicly attacked by special interests. This is where ministers and their departments either hang together or hang separately. Public opinion polls chart a minister's progress. Becoming a major embarrassment to the government is not usually a passport to a brilliant ministerial career. But being obliged to let a bill die is also no testament to effectiveness.

The point is that opinion polls, not MPs, moderate the legislative process at every stage except the technical stuff that nobody watches. What they do look at — smooth market-making to prepare opinion for some measure through release of new studies, a couple of ministerial sound bites, or the haranguing of question period— provide no guidance whatever on how we are actually governed or how the system has evolved. And if news coverage did provide that information, only those who know it already would probably bother to watch.

None of this emerged overnight. The system is an evolutionary response to the social forces that push and pull on our institutions. The critical problem now is that it has provoked a crisis of representation.

The crisis of representation is simply that the different elements of society feel they can improve their access to power by changing the way they are represented. So-called visible minorities believe that their special causes can only be adequately represented by visible minority representatives. Some women's groups believe that legislatures need to have 50 per cent female representation to reflect the population as a whole (something the Canadian voters achieved for the Tories within their party overnight.) Regional interests feel under-represented unless they have a piece of cabinet proportional to their population, and so on. The problem is compounded by a first-past-the post majority system that generates a majority in the commons — and thus government power — with a minority of votes, a situation that worsens the more parties that run. So, for example, the Conservatives got the same amount of votes as the Bloc Quebecois. But the BQ got 54 seats and the PCs only two.

Nonetheless, offsetting these problems, the system is effective in one respect: it is hostile to change. Generating the policy outputs is very difficult because of all the constituencies that must be consulted.

At the root of the representation problem are two major fallacies. One is that the more people you consult, the more closely your product will reflect the general interest. This is the well-known fallacy of composition, committed whenever you assume the whole is only the sum of its parts. A second fallacy is less well-known: it is the assumption that majority support can be reached over a range of measures by democratic vote. While there is no reason it cannot occur, the belief that it MUST occur was exploded in strictly logical terms by Kenneth Arrow, in his famous "impossibility theorem", a staple of decision-theory courses. This theorem shows that without the guiding hand of a player who is more equal than the others, a majority will exist for all alternatives in an array of choices, even if some of those alternatives are contrary to others. These two theorems show that on strictly logical grounds, no adequate representation can be possible. It's another way of saying that trust, not accountability, is the basic problem in democracies. In other words, today's crisis of representativeness is a crisis of trust. Trust, of course, is the flip side of accountability. Accountability cannot be perfect, nor does it need to be. Accountability only needs to be good enough to promote trust.

Now our argument throughout is that government as we knew it — the military defender and the last resort provider of economic security — is no longer credible in any guise, because the world has evolved so as to make those functions impossible. If we expect governments never to abandon those roles as traditionally conceived, we are bound to be disappointed and disbelieving. The safe is empty and putting up more guards will be to no avail. The problem is what can be done to help government regain the trust of its citizens.

The logic in this book has been that the technology exists to remove the barriers that exist at various critical junctures in society between those who pay and those who provide. Applying that logic to public representation will yield prescriptions such as the following:

The erosion of parliament's power to scrutinize can be overcome by letting the public choose the programs it is prepared to fund. Beyond the basic minimum of services that would otherwise be subject to free riding (National defence, infrastructure, etc.) we ought to be able to vote on where we want our tax money to go. This could be done on every tax return. In addition to the line where we say how much we are paying, we could also check off programs, envelopes or policy areas where we would prefer to allocate our money, like United Way does and as referenda do in some American states. The public could choose.

So far, we've been concentrating on national and provincial governments. But as we've argued throughout, their actual capacity to add value to Canada is steeply diminished in a global economy. What has not diminished, however, is the need for municipal government services. We still live in cities, we increasingly work at home in cities,— our schools are mainly in cities, and the new telecommunications services will be delivered through the local loop that serves our neighbourhood —again an affair of cities.

A major determining factor in the economic viability of cities is their air, surface transport and telecommunications links with other cities. Another is their degree of social peace and lack of crime, a function of the effectiveness of municipal social services to provide alternatives for youth. And the list could go on.

As the new economy erodes the relevance of national governments, it increases the importance of effective municipal government. Right now Canada generates most of its wealth in cities, most of its taxes in cities and consumes most public services in cities. Yet cities have only one tax base — property taxes — and that is potentially the most distorting tax of all. It makes no sense to send a dollar of taxes to Ottawa and have it come back as 70 cents worth of services that send cities into spasms of despair over how to keep up quality of life. It makes more sense to shift most of the tax space to metropolitan areas and let the citizenry vote on how much they will send to higher levels of government. The discipline on cities? Competition.

This is less radical than it sounds. In practice, that is already going on, but to the detriment of Canadian living standards. Tax competition between Montreal and its suburb, Laval, is ensuring that Laval attracts clusters of new industries while Montreal is left with the costs of vestigial industrial society: the homeless, the single mothers, ageing industrial plant and an overpaid civil service and police force.

Ottawa is going through the same competition with Nepean and Kanata. Indeed, every Canadian city is warring over scarce property tax dollars to the detriment of our critical municipal infrastructure, a source of major international comparative advantage. Transferring tax points would help solve this problem at a time when federal and provincial levels of government are less and less relevant in any case.

A municipally-based tax structure would encourage a tiering of communities in which services offered, tax rates and services demanded were equated at the margin. Interestingly, the effect of such a system would also be to enhance property values in poorer neighbourhoods with lower taxes — and, overall, ensure that cities for the first time had enough resources to maintain and enhance

Work at Home Hits Critical Mass

Roughly 40% of American workers — 48 million people — do part of their job away from the office. The accessibility and affordability of high performance technologies makes this possible.

That, plus lifestyle, workplace and demographic changes translate into a booming number of people working at home.

Working at home continues to grow. According to Link Resources, a market research firm that specializes in this field, in the past 4 years, the number of people who work at home jumped 53%, from 27 million in 1989 to 41 million in 1993.

Personal computers can now be found in 31% of all American homes, up 26.6% from last year. Link Resources says PC penetration for work-at-home households is 58%, while that for small businesses is 67%. But according to a survey conducted by Home Office Computing magazine, the percentage of small businesses that own desktop computers is closer to 100%. Ownership of other electronic devices was found as follows:

Answering machine	83%	Mouse or track ball	70%
Dot-matrix printer	66%	Cordless phone	44%
Laser printer	40%	Modem	40%
Fax board or modem	35%	Fax machine	29%
Copier	29%	Multiline phone	27%
Cellular phone	20%	Scanner	17%
Notebook or laptop computer	17%		

Home Office Computing magazine readership survey shows that 98% of those working at home say they're happier running their businesses than working for someone else. Even more significant was the finding that working from home has lost its stigma throughout the business world.

Finally: if you commute an hour a day to work and an hour back, you're spending 500 hours a year in the car. That's the equivalent of 62.5 work days, or 12.5 work weeks. As we head toward a billion cars world-wide, the desire to choose the road less travelled can only grow stronger.

From "Futurescan"

superior infrastructure —another plus for the country in attracting foreign investors.

Conclusion

This chapter argues that the modern state suffers a crisis in representation that at its root reflects a number of things. One is the automatic breakdown in trust between governors and governed when the state continues to pretend it can fulfil responsibilities like defence and provider of economic welfare that it can in reality no longer provide. Another is the erosion of parliament to scrutinize and control public spending. Letting people indicate on their tax returns the programs they wish to fund would stiffen MPs scrutinizing.

Beyond that, the argument is made that the new global economy makes municipal services relatively more important and that this level, not the national level, should be the level of priority tax jurisdiction. Cities generate the wealth and consume the product. Healing the rifts that divide us should start there.

8

JOBS, JOBS, JOBS

The economy has been out
of recession for more than a
year, and is now producing
more goods and services,
and the value of GDP is
rising.

But unemployment's at 11
per cent and there are still
lots of layoffs. It is these
two facts together that
make people believe the
recession's not over.

Observers, including US president Bill Clinton, now talk about the difference between "the facts" and the "feel good" factor. Indeed, President Clinton has modified the official definition of a recession by saying it won't be over until the economy starts creating jobs.

Beneath the aggregate number of 11 per cent, are several other facts. For example, about a third of all the males in the workforce are actually unemployed, many of them studying, albeit with no concrete outcome in sight. They don't know if there will there be jobs for them when their courses end. Meanwhile, part time work is increasing — but the pay and benefits are less good.

Defining Unemployment

Full employment does not mean zero unemployment. In the ordinary course of events, people move from job to job, and often are unemployed for brief periods of time. Economists call that frictional unemployment. Also, when people are unemployed because their skills aren't appropriate, that's called structural unemployment. Economists think both are more or less inevitable. So the full employment rate of unemployment, or the "natural" rate of unemployment is a number that's greater than zero. That number is not always the same number. During the 1950s and 60s, it was commonly held that this unavoidable minimum unemployment was 3 or 4%. Today, Canadian economists think it's 7 or 8%. So economists would say the economy was fully employed if the unemployment rate was 7 or 8% instead of 11% — a million people unemployed instead of a million and a half.

Where have the jobs gone and what can we do about it? Conventional economics looks at the job market as a problem in supply and demand. But everyone, economists included, recognizes there's more to it than that. If we follow the approach we've used so far, the first step would be to face up to what the economy really looks like. Here, as in every national economy, as writers about the economy have observed for 100 years or more, there are really at least three economies, linked to each other to be sure, but which play by somewhat different rules.

First of all, there's the economy dominated by large companies. In Canada, the top 158 companies account for half the country's output. The top 20 companies account for about 40 per cent of that, or about 20 per cent of the nation's sales. The biggest car companies, the phone companies and their equipment suppliers, some food companies, hydro, whisky makers, banks and insurance companies pretty much make up the top 20. But the top Canadian firms only account for about 2 million jobs. The rest — 8 or 9 million — are supplied by medium to small enterprise.

The top companies are now encountering competition that they were unused to dealing with a generation ago. They are downsizing, shedding jobs and making headlines as they do so. But the medium and small firms are hardy competitors, having always had to hustle to make their payrolls. Employment is growing in this sector, but mainly in the form of part-time employment, so as to get around payroll taxes and other regulations imposed by federal and provincial governments.

Two American financial institution - Citicorp and Fleet Financial allow customers to buy and sell mutual funds through their automated tell machines (ATMs).

The allure is obvious: ATMs are heavily used by baby boomers, perhaps the hottest prospects for banks eager to sell mutual funds. And the machines represent a tempting distribution network.

Using ATMs has the added benefit of reminding consumers that mutual funds are part of the bank and not a separate business.

From the Files of *The American Banker*

There is as well, a third, informal, sector. This is growing as the top sector shrinks. Some estimates now place it around 25 per cent of national output: especially in home renovations, tobacco products, alcoholic beverages used in the restaurant business, and many personal services. Despite a slump in housing starts, this sector is booming, as anyone knows who's tried to get her house fixed recently.

Statisticians and economists do not consider all these elements when they make employment policy. In fact, they limit themselves to considering big and small business as the areas to influence in order to create full-time jobs with benefits. Nor, because of their quasi-Newtonian market models, do they seriously consider the web of interactions linking these sectors. Yet the key to understanding and finally solving the jobs problem lies in figuring out the way the "web" actually works. Make no mistake. When it works, it works very well. In the 1980s, between recessions, something like 10 per cent of the work force used to change jobs every year. Research shows that most jobs are filled by word of mouth — personal connections, the way we relate to each other, the web, the network. Even when changing jobs meant inter-company transfers, those transfers usually occurred as cohorts of associates moved around an organization and so around the country. So the question is, what's happened? Why can't these nets work like they used to and absorb the changes going on in the top two sectors?

What's happening is that the web is getting more and more people into the informal, third sector. What's happened in the top two sectors is well-captured by the industry models used by Michael Porter to account for competitiveness. Effectively, new technology and tumbling trade barriers have made it cheaper for firms to out-source on a world basis some things they used to buy or make internally in each region. Another change is that new technologies are replacing managers whose main job was just to transmit information without adding substantial value to it.

The consequence: the home market served by domestic suppliers effectively shrinks under the pressure of foreign competitors. The networks that used to absorb these changes are suddenly devalued by their lack of international contacts to compensate for the loss of useful domestic ones. You may have a great product, but if your chief customer decides to buy abroad, then you've got to sell abroad to pick up the sale you lost. Far too few Canadians have the contacts needed to do that without major new spending — so they just absorb the loss by downsizing themselves. When you have seasoned professionals out of work in their 50s, drawing down their RRSPs 10 years too soon, you have also vastly increased the market open to the third, informal sector.

Add to this the pressure on our social programs as the third sector expands, and you have new taxes squeezing the absorptive capacity of small businesses (in addition to pressures of technological change and foreign competition). The best managed companies remain competitive under these conditions, even increasing their international sales. Everyone else has an adjustment to make.

Canada's knee-jerk reaction to this has been to treat these changes as cyclical rather than structural. Our policy-makers tell us that the jobs will come back again once the "economy turns around". But the economy won't "turn around". Instead, it is already recreating itself in a different mode, one in which the informal sector is absorbing the adjustments imposed by the changes at the top.

Reasonably, you might think that the policy response would be to simultaneously encourage this sector in order to help people make these adjustments, and to help create the new international networks our enterprises need. Instead, however, the policy has mainly attacked (and is gearing up for a more lethal assault on) the informal survival systems that make up the third sector. Among current policy-makers, these systems, rhetorically anyway, are presumed to offer alternatives so attractive that they are undermining the reentry to the workforce of qualified people — as if qualified people would prefer to live on UIC and work for tips. True, the government also offers training programs designed to make the work force more flexible and productive. But the question always arises, training for what? Canada has skill shortages to be sure. But most training programs presume those jobs will be available to a newly-trained person, rather than starting with a job to train for.

Excerpts from the notes of William Bridges

The concept of a "job" has taken several evolutionary steps since Shakespeare's time. Until fairly recently, people didn't have jobs — they did jobs. They worked just as hard, but they worked on a cluster of tasks, in a variety of locations, on a schedule set by the sun and the needs of the day.

The word originally meant a hunk of something... so its first meaning was something you did to a hunk of something. Thereafter, it became a project or unit of work, as in 'order it in job lots';

- any piece of work, as in 'he's an odd jobs man'; anything done for hire — 'that's his job'; and, as industrial organization demanded it, a regular set of duties, with regular pay and regular hours and,

- a fixed place in the organization's structure — 'I lost my job'.

There's plenty of evidence that we're coming full circle: the conditions — the industrial age — that created 'jobs' is coming to an end.

The fact remains, the key ingredient in getting a job is the network. The adjustment the economy is undergoing has destroyed many previously useful networks. Getting into government training programs has become a loop in the informal economy.

Failure to solve this problem of unemployment or worker adjustment, call it what you will, imposes greater costs than just the sheer numbers of individuals involved. The threat of persistent unemployment erodes confidence in the future and in the soundness of the system as a whole. A problem, too, is the issue of time. There are many reasons to be optimistic in the long run. Our managers are becoming more international and our larger companies are increasing their links to foreign markets. New networks are emerging with international orientation. The real policy question is, what about the shorter term adjustment ?

To be effective, policy has to reflect the emerging reality, not the disappearing one. The new economy will offer security of employment — but not job security. You'll always find work if you keep on top of change. But you won't keep the same job.

William Bridges, continued ...

Organizations are not patterns of jobs, they are a great wide field of work needing to be done. Those 9 to 5 boxes on an organizational chart, with regular duties and salaries, are rigid solutions to an elastic problem. When the 'work that needs to be done' changes constantly, we cannot constantly be writing new job descriptions. 'Jobs' are no longer socially adaptive artefacts, and they are going the way of the Dodo.

Thus, new firms operate with cross-trained work teams where job descriptions have ceased to exist. "Virtual" corporations, which come together to do a specific project and are linked by phone and fax, are already reality. There's no shortage of part-time work.

A shift in focus from a 'job' to 'work that needs to be done' also means a huge shift in what it means to be employed. We need to think anew about all facets of the job that will disappear when it does - pensions, security, benefits, social identity, and the structure of our everyday lives.

In fact, you'll probably change careers three or four times. What's more, the new economy shifts responsibility for making these changes onto the individual worker. What you know and whom you know are the best guarantees of a long, productive working life. Now clearly, to make that effective, policy has to make retraining a real option. As for the question, retraining for what?, the answer is, "For stuff I need to know so I can do what I'm likely to be asked to do next — because I can see what's happening in my network."

Experience shows networks to be more effective than centralized bureaucracies. The real key to a solution is to strengthen networks. And part of that strengthening has to be to make training accessible easily, and virtually on demand.

A particularly good way is to float the underground economy to the surface. Cut taxes on the poor, eliminate payroll taxes on small business. That will help a bit on the demand side. But more is required.

A major need is cooperative education programs in emerging trades, combined with some instruction on how to offer those trades as an independent supplier — as an entrepreneur, rather than as an employee. In such programs, participants work with firms as part of a training program. The firm gets free, well-trained labour. The candidate gets some experience and a chance to show what s/he can do. In the course of the job, new networks can be established and old ones strengthened. Community colleges and a major emphasis on distance learning are other essential ingredients.

Right now, these are almost impossible to deliver on, because of very serious bottlenecks — the result of interests groups with a hammerlock on the future. Classroom teachers fear they'll be laid off if distance learning grows, unions want to certify who takes what courses, government functionaries clinging to ideas of tripartism want to insert themselves into a top-down process. Telecommunications regulations impede the introduction of state of the art technology.

The interaction of Canadian policy and institutions is too slow, too rigid, too expensive and too restrictive. The things cited above are needed now and should be offered on a consenting basis between employees and their employers. Often courses need only provide short updates and refreshers on skills employees already have. You don't need elaborate tax breaks, extensive certification or links to UIC to achieve this. Just expand the student loan fund and let all repayments be tax deductible once the student starts earning. Most of the machinery to do this is in place, but we've hamstrung ourselves by too much red tape and organizational log jams. We've got the legs but we've fixed it so we can't use 'em.

Ohmigosh, some policy wonk will now ask, won't that program leave the informal sector intact? The answer is yes. That is, it will leave free of hassle the single mothers, the welfare recipients, the people who for one reason or another are unable to work full time but who can find part-time employment for cash. People will move in and out of that sector as their circumstances change.

But the great contradictions — so that a middle class professional with two children can do better on welfare than with a taxed earned income — will be largely eliminated by the tax cut. And the accessibility of new knowledge in the precise doses needed to get and keep a job — will keep people trying to get back to work.

What about strengthening international networks? The cheapest way to do this is by changing our telecommunications policy and letting people have ready access to computers and modems. The $5 billion helicopter deal (including contingency fees to lobbyists because high-paid bureaucrats aren't trusted to make the "correct" decision) could have given every Canadian household a modem-equipped computer loaded with software and ready to rock and roll throughout the continent and the world.

A Strategy to Cure Job Market Stickiness

The "churn" in Canada's fully-employed labour market is seven per cent — an indication that even under full employment, millions of people change jobs every year. What enables them to do this is the network of friends and professional contacts they have who identify new opportunities and who may even encourage the change. When the economy goes into reverse, these networks are still useful because they provide the hope and impetus people need to recover their jobs when the pace of economic activity turns around. But when an economy restructures, there are major problems. The changing job mix devalues not only the jobs but the networks of personal contacts that accompanies them. When environmental disaster puts the fish plant workers out of business, when a technology shift puts engineers on hold, countless tiny civilizations are wiped out and investments of time, feeling, energy and commitment are destroyed. The full accounting includes the emotional and psychological damage to human beings. What's even more shocking, there's no need for it.

The major problem in the job market is its stickiness: people are encouraged to cling to old jobs even as they are obsolescing. And then they are encouraged to wait for those jobs to recur — or else to retrain drastically for "new jobs" AFTER a devastating shutdown. In a better managed economy, the emphasis would be on retraining for emerging jobs while people were employed. An aspect of that training would be the creation of new networks of contacts so that transitions could be managed smoothly.

As presently organized, our labour market can't do this. The big business sector is cumbersome. Unions see new members of their trade as potential competitors who will lower wages, so they have no inducement to smooth transitions of that sort. Employers also view training for new jobs as destabilizing for their labour force and potentially costly. Governments see themselves as the underwriters, facilitators or even suppliers of the training, with the consent of the others. Result: the interests of the individuals is lost — she can still take a course at the community college or university, but it will be at their convenience, not hers and her risk. One common recommendation is to institute a training tax such that employees would have an entitlement to upgrade their skills in any organization or else the employer would be liable to pay the tax. The tax is seen as the transfer of funds from the unvirtuous to the virtuous and is typically recommended by people who see taxes as socially improving. The trouble with this approach is that taxes represent a wedge between the payer and the beneficiary. It simply substitutes one distortion for another.

Small business, usually (and mistakenly) seen as necessarily less capital intensive than big business, is rightly one of the chief opponents of a training tax. And, despite the lack of formal training in many small companies, in fact, a great many well-managed small companies put a lot of effort into how they train their employees and will make every effort to help them upgrade their personal qualifications. Usually, however, this is through increased flexibility, rather than a transfer of resources. There remains the feeling that if a valued employee leaves, even if it's by outgrowing the job, the loser is the business that nurtured the employee. Thus, measured in time, money and risk, training again imposes a burden chiefly upon the trainee. At the informal level, the situation is worsened by the fact that once unemployed, getting training is many times easier than getting another job. So job training becomes a way station on the road to benefits, supplemented with work in the shadows.

The problem nevertheless remains one of information and contacts. The principle problem is networks: how to make them effective. The federal government has recognized this and has established a computer network designed to link job seekers and employers nation-wide. But it is an after-the-fact solution, based on catch-up, not reinforcing active networks.

A more pro-active approach would be to open up the one demand-driven network that remains viable in Canada for almost everybody, working or not: Interac — the bank card line. Just about every household has a bank card. That card is linked to financial records that includes education and job history. The same network also links corporate bank cards with similar information in their credit files. This network could be configured to match would-be job changers with companies with expansion plans and similar qualifications. It could also be used to point out to card holders where an upgrade in training could qualify them for higher income opportunities about to emerge in the country.

From the files of the Federal Reserve, RAM Research Corp.; *Futurescan*

In any one day, about 85% of all dollar payments are made in cash, but they represent less than 1% of the total value of all transactions. Electronic transfers account for about 2% of all payments, but represent fully 83% of the total value of all dollar transactions world wide — a stunning $1.7 trillion a day.

The number of credit cards in Canada and the US is approaching 300 million, up from just over 200 million 5 years ago.

Should the banks play this clearing house role? Why not? The banks are among the chief losers from the current job market lumpiness. They must mediate the cost when networks and other investments lose their value. And it would be a viable-fee-for-service business. Plus, there would be no barrier between service and beneficiary as the tax system would impose.

What about the trainers? Probably they borrow from the bank like the rest of us. Your friendly ATM, triggered by your bank card and PIN could help you find the right trainer for your needs as well. By increasing the economies of scope on the bank networks, all members of the network would benefit.

What about the underground economy? Improving the lumpiness in the job market would reduce the claims on the system, thus reducing taxes and permitting the "black" economy to come out of the shadows.

The Bank Act provides a way for banks to enter this business through a special corporation. But current privacy laws, competition law and other aspects of financial regulation act as major deterrents to this kind of innovation. Typical of the way we hold ourselves back, ever faithful to the old ways, awaiting their return.

9

Managing the Paper Burden

There is one class of
strategic change that the
country is groping towards
and which we need to make
explicit and even promote:
TEXT MANAGEMENT.
This is perhaps the place
for active government
intervention. In effect, we
need to revamp totally the
way we deal with TEXT in
our economic system.

S ounds a little much to say that changing the way we handle text will go a long way towards fixing up the Canadian economy. But just think of the amount of text the system goes over every day. New laws, changed regulations, a flood of memos and correspondence, specialized files like medical records, various kinds of instructions from recipes to repair manuals, stacks and stacks of text per day per person, employed or unemployed.

Information overload

Computers have already vastly increased our capability to process text. But they have not as yet enabled us to understand text any better. In fact, if anything, they may have made things worse simply by enabling us to be less clear the first time (because we can always fix it later) and because it is so easy to distribute text electronically. CD-ROM storage disks also include extensive search and retrieve capabilities and CD-I (interactive CD-ROMs) enhance this capability even more.

Y et even as we move into these technologies or install our networks on the job, our text management is still a drag on the system. Why? because although we can access documents, transmit documents to addressable locations, etc., we still are not taking advantage of the available technology to create so-called "living documents".

A living document works like this. It sits on your computer, but it is network aware. That is, parts of it are or can be found in other computers on your network. The document is self-updating, self-customizing, and self-activating. Whenever someone on the network generates a change to the document, the living document signals that it has been changed and shows you how and where. The document is self-customizing in that it will show you only the parts you've indicated you want to see. The document is self-activating in that if actions are called for by a certain date or time, it will either take the action itself or alert you to the actions that need to be done. The secret to building documents like this has been with us for a long time — hypertext.

Hypertext,

an idea that goes back some 30 years, is text organized so that words and ideas can be linked by connotation and association. So you can skip around it, looking for different references to particular themes and ideas. Most of us don't organize our text files in hypertext, and most of us who have computers are not interconnected. Instead, if we are linked to computers in an office or we use electronic data bases, we check in to a file server—the computer with the data we want, find what we want and then log out again. Like turning on the tap, filling the kettle and turning off the tap.

An example of interconnection is the Internet — the international network of academics and researchers that has some 30 million potential users world wide. Searching on the Internet allows you to search all the nodes at once for what you want. You can also post whatever you want so that anybody else on the network who's interested can find it.

Another example: think of documents as divided into two classes — those our economic, political and legal systems demand and those designed for people, a useful distinction made by Russell Lipton, a Connecticut based multimedia expert. Updates to laws and regulations, to product specifications, to draft legislation and other government documents, new reports on specific subjects — are all system- designed documents. By organizing them in hypertext, they can be made available to network clients as automatic updates, customized information and triggers to certain kinds of action. The receptors or clients' programs can themselves ensure that the documents contain the pertinent information.

We remain a text-based society. Text and the sequences it sets up control what we do. We can improve on the sequencing and bring professional and other services up to the standards of agile production by managing our national paper flow in this way.

Dividing the flow into documents for the system and documents for people; creating documents that are network sensitive and can be assembled from several "servers". Ensuring automatic updating and automatic customizing and self-activation would free managers from the demands of managing a paper flow to managing the organization.

Communities could start urban freenets with Internet access. Freenets are just local bulletin boards that also let you send and receive electronic mail. Freenets enable municipal government to post documents electronically and to receive documents electronically, avoiding downtime and telephone callbacks, etc. It would even enable town hall forums to be held irrespective of time and place.

We could hypertext government documents and put them on networks that can be accessed through freenets. This would enable the creation of living documents about urban developments — new rules, new taxes, new zoning proposals, results and notices of meetings. We could create a national e-mail system. It's no accident that Britain's industrial leadership was achieved at about the same time it introduced the first mail system with a standardized rate structure. This meant that information could be broadcast simultaneously over the whole country at the rate of the fastest available transport. A national e-mail system would provide that capability at light speed.

Taking corporate voice mail and e-mail systems together—most of which can be reached by outside providers—we probably are very close already. Households can get the same through the phone company (voice mail), Bell's Inet 2000 and e-mail through freenets or commercial services like Compuserve. Within the workplace, these capabilities are already very widespread. But you still can't send a message to someone at a simple address. You need to know too much to really make the most of our technological capabilities. A little standardization would go a long way to resolving this problem.

Taking these few small steps to use to the fullest the technology we now have would dramatically reduce the costs of doing business in Canada. Its development would allow smaller companies and governments to establish national grids for ordering, suppliers, shipping, business documents, permits, instant up-dates of laws, regulations, repair manuals and other customer support.

A surprising amount of infrastructure is already in place and more is on the way. Canadian companies are pretty well equipped with local and wide area networks: they are widely "LANned and WANned", with file servers automatically updating overnight.

Quite a lot of government information is already available electronically, including Supreme Court of Canada decisions and environmental information. Redesigning the documents for network awareness as well as cross-linking—rescripting to give them life— can be done as they are updated.

Nova Scotia Power Inc.'s entire power grid is electronically controlled with information transmitted to computers using telecommunications.

The Energy Control Centre, near Halifax, monitors the amount of power being produced at more than 30 generating stations bringing units on and off as needed.

"Telecommunications allows us to optimize power production. Without it, millions of dollars would be wasted from using the wrong generator at the wrong time," says David Gibbs, telecommunications specialist for the investor-owned provincial electrical utility.

The system is designed to automatically switch out faulty electrical equipment to prevent the system-wide blackouts over large areas that would otherwise occur.

Many power utilities are also investigating automatic meter reading systems, which transmit usage data directly from customer homes.

"We're continuing to look at it," Mr. Gibbs says. "While we currently have people read the meter, the information that they collect is recorded on hand-held terminals and transmitted to central computers for billing. In addition, at selected sites we are remotely collecting data not for billing purposes but to track consumption patterns. This is invaluable data for rate and market analysis. "

From the Files of an ROB Special Report

What's the easiest way to understand the importance of this shift? Linking the national document flow in electronic living documents would alter the basic structures of everyday life in Canada in a way not seen since the introduction of universal schooling.

If government is looking for an information age mega-project to kick-start the economy, this is it. It's better than fixing roads, and work after the initial start up would continue.

Look at the interventions for which the Canadian government still is happy to take some credit: the building of the railroad, the creation of a national airline, of a national broadcasting system, of a medicare system, even of the Wheat Board. Each of these in their day went beyond mere counter-cyclical spending. They upgraded the sophistication of the nation in a way the private sector could not do at the time. These changes gave Canada a sustained advantage over its competitors. So would the creation of an interconnected living document network. The real value from the system would come from starting in the city halls, putting municipal documents into the system for people to access — permits, licenses, bill and tax payments, school board info, etc. Provincial documents would come next; finally, the system-related documentation at the federal level. These could be made accessible either directly or through community freenets using Internet access.

A second change — greatly improving management process —would flow from the successful implementation of the network. Small companies would have access to vast amounts of information about other companies including potential business opportunities. Companies would be encouraged to form networks and partnerships and compete for global business. The virtual corporation would move many steps closer to reality.

Consider the effects on quality management. Companies without programs would easily find

Transportation

While the transportation industry is seldom thought of as being on the leading edge of high tech, more and more companies are depending on telecommunications for their survival.

Truckers have long been fans of citizen band radios, which allow them to talk to others within a three-kilometre radius. Increasingly their bosses are turning to telecommunications to communicate with drivers, track shipments and even monitor truck movements and speed.

While radio communications have long been used for trucks operating in a local basis, their use for long-distance communications was limited by cost and restricted availability. Consequently, long-haul operators used to depend mainly on the truckers calling in at prearranged times along their route.

One of the first courier companies to recognize the value of telecommunications in transportation was Federal Express Corp. of Memphis.

"Half of what our customers are paying for is delivery," says David Bronszak, president of Federal Express Canada. "The other half is information."

Mobile communications combined with Federal Express's scanning and tracking technology gave the company a major competitive advantage and sent Purolator Courier Ltd. and Canada Post Corp. scrambling to introduce similar systems.

But the advances in communications have not just affected large companies. J. S. Crawford and Son, a 30-truck fleet based in Toronto, is one of the early users of mobile satellite to provide data links with its drivers.

Trucks are equipped with satellite antennae and drivers are given portable terminals on which they can send and receive typed messages. They also have pagers for when they leave the truck.

"We were spending $2,000 to $3,000 per month on cellular for each driver. Now instead of a $3 call, we can exchange short messages with the driver for less than 50 cents. They still have to call in for some problems but over the past three months we've cut down on our long-distance costs dramatically," says John Crawford, president of the company.

From the Files of an ROB Special Report

companies with them and discover how to manage the empowerment of their own workforce. The spread of knowledge and awareness would upgrade the national business base. Above all, the coordination and management of many small businesses to generate returns matching those of single larger businesses, would be greatly facilitated.

The technology to accomplish this is readily available. The contention throughout this argument is that Canada has changed economically, socially and politically over the last few years, primarily as the result of massive world wide investments in process technology. To capture the benefits of this investment, companies have had to evolve towards flatter structures, more outsourcing, the development of partnerships and alliances and now networks.

But the market does not drive all society or for that matter all of the economy. Habits, inertia, and a simple preference for the familiar can set limits to what the market will change. It looks like those limits have been reached in Canada. Any further economic change will be incremental and minor — or else explosive, because of pent-up pressures.

Yet before we totally draw the line, we ought to make this additional set of changes — in a sense an investment in social process to match the investment already made in production processes. Managing the national text flow to the maximum permitted by our technologies would carry us to another possibility curve, transform the structures of everyday life and enable us to clear up most of the remaining obstacles to once more achieving sustained competitive advantage.

It could be argued that this change will also overwhelm the networks designed to carry the information, just as urban freenets are pretty much overwhelmed now. Too many callers, constant busy signals, or so much demand on the file server computers that they can't keep up.

Perhaps strangely, we believe that crowding the limits of the existing networks with user demand would be a good outcome. Because then the question whether a viable market exists for connection to already existing fibre optic cable with huge information-carrying capacity would be answered affirmatively. Enough commercial pressure might be created to end the funding squabbles and enable the completion of an electronic superhighway in advance of the US.

Here's the last thought. We don't need to wait for the superhighway before we make the changes. Rather, we need to push today's possibilities to the limits, and then tomorrow will look a lot better.

We have the technology. All that's lacking is the will.

Pratt & Whitney Canada Inc., a world leader in small gas turbine engines for business and commuter aircraft and helicopters with customers in more than 150 countries, operates round-the-clock customer service lines offering technical, marketing and commercial support.

The company uses high-speed networks to link computer assisted drafting and design systems in separate locations. It is also a leader in the field of computer integrated manufacturing. A company spokesmen says they don't do much videoconferencing because transmission costs are too high and the service is not widely available. Telecommunications has allowed Pratt & Whitney to reduce product cycles and be more reactive to the market.

Increasingly the company is entering into joint development and manufacturing agreements with European and Asian partners because of the extremely high cost of producing engines on its own. *From the files of an ROB Special Report*

The grocery business is about to go high tech to implement something called "efficient consumer response". ECR is the name given to the process of completely re-engineering the existing supply chain to replenish the consumer's purchases at the lowest possible cost.

Four recent studies — by FMI/McKinsey, Coca-Cola Research Council, Arthur Andersen and by the industry told the industry it couldn't survive if it didn't change. The basic industry operations of replenishing inventory at the store and the warehouse were antiquated, inadequate and inefficient. Unnecessary inventories at various levels of the distribution system and antiquated systems of buying, selling and promoting, were adding billions of dollars of cost to the consumer who now had other alternatives to supermarket shopping.

The good news, said these studies, is that the technology exists to move into 21st century replenishment. All that's necessary is to change the way they do business and the internal culture.

ECR will mean continuous replenishment by the supplier at the distribution centre and continuous replenishment by the supplier and distributor at the store. Ultimately, it will bring continuous replenishment to the household. Studies estimate that implementing ECR would squeeze US$30 billion waste from existing supply arrangements.

From the files of *Supermarket Business Magazine*

"Having the right goods in the right place at the right time at the right price is the key to success," says Wayne East, vice-president for information services with National Grocers Co. Ltd., a subsidiary of Loblaw Cos. Ltd. of Toronto.

"Telecommunications helps us do it." In an industry battered by the recession, free trade and cross-border shopping, many retailers are struggling just to survive.

Point-of-sale terminals streamline the checkout process in most department stores, drugstores and supermarkets. Increasingly they are linked to inventory control and merchandising systems and even to suppliers. Electronic data interchange (EDI), a standard for transmitting more than 200 trading documents - purchase orders, shipping information, bills of lading, invoices and more - is reducing the labour costs and time associated with processing transactions.

But more critically, EDI is also the key to managing inventories and cash more effectively. Unsold goods sitting in warehouses and stores represent a huge cost and product shortages are lost sales. "Now we are pushing to link up with more suppliers. Eventually, we would like the system to automatically place orders when inventory falls before a certain level," Mr. East says.

While the benefits of electronic data interchange have been recognized for grocers, there is potentially even more benefit to retailers selling soft goods such as clothing. When they overstock, the risk is far greater that they will be left holding the bag.

In the current economic environment, many companies have a short-term orientation and feel they cannot afford the investment in technologies such as EDI. But, says Mel Fruitman, vice-president of the Retail Council of Canada, "if they want to stay alive and thrive, they can't afford not to."

From the files of an ROB Special Report

10

Reposition Education

For years, pundits of the new economy have been pointing out the educational possibilities of interactive distance learning created by new technology. Exciting as is the technology on the drawing board, it's also a fact that the technology we have NOW is better, cheaper and easier to use than educators could have imagined even in the mid-1980s.

At a time when Canada's economy is transformed by massive restructuring, clear and positive management thought is more in demand than ever. What is needed, everyone agrees, is a new proactive attitude of searching out and tackling new markets. And in response to new realities, business people are looking for information and training to help them sail before the new trade winds.

While long-established institutions of business teaching are often slow to respond to changes, the less traditional ones are quick to develop new courses. Across Canada there are many such organizations offering business knowledge and even educational credits. In Ontario, among the most prominent are CJRT Open College, TVOntario, and the University of Toronto's School of Continuing Studies.

Open College offers university credit courses by radio, audio cassette and written correspondence. Open College also provides a number of services and aids, such as student co-ordinators, orientation workshops, study skills workshops and writing and research tutors.

The other notable source of business education on the air is TVOntario's division of Distance Learning. Business titles include: Business Strategies for Growth, the Business of Managing Professionals, Marketing for Everyone, and How Will You Manage? The programs are available on VHS cassettes with a companion text.

The University of Toronto, through its School of Continuing Studies, is another provider of business education that's off the beaten track.

The School offers computer-based training, videotape lessons, state-of-the-art interactive video delivery, as well as live instruction to adults who have neither the time nor the inclination to sit in classrooms. And, like TVO, the school will be developing tailor-made courses to help train employees by "distance learning" at a company's place of business.

From the files of an *ROB Special Report*

Yet, perhaps surprisingly, very little use has been made of these applications for actual teaching.

Some universities have embraced the new technologies and sought to create electronic teaching networks. There is an electronic university network and about a dozen universities, mainly in North America and the U.K., able to offer degrees in computer- and television-taught courses. Many other services are made available into specific classes by individual school boards throughout Canada and the United States. Satellite TV and community TV offer TV university courses, Videotron in Montreal has services designed to improve command of French and English. Among scholars themselves, the embrace has been firmer. Most researchers now collaborate over Internet. But all this activity involves only a handful of enthusiasts. The impact has hardly been revolutionary. At levels other than university, the uptake of new technologies has been even less enthusiastic—despite sometimes heroic efforts of individual teachers and boards.

The reason the full potential of the technology has not been reached is that it's not being exploited — schools create their own environment and break down the walls to the outside world only with great difficulty.

For one thing, educational institutions operate on a different time frame than the rest of us. Universities in particular, still medieval institutions at heart, have changed their subjects of instruction, but not their method in centuries. Research is primarily an individual, craft activity, a far cry from the current industry practice or even that of the average television documentary news team. Teaching is firmly geared to the agricultural calendar of 26 weeks between harvest and spring planting, divided in the middle by Christmas. Somewhere, long, long ago, it was decided that subjects should be divided into 13 week sessions of three hours each, and so on.

In a recent 10 year period in Canada, there have been 40 expert studies of, and 600 recommendations for fixing the education system. There has been no action. We have the advanced telecommunications to deliver lifelong learning and training. But with our country depressed, divided and in disarray, we do nothing.

We invest more per capita than any other country except Japan; we pay our teachers 40 per cent more than those in the United States. (Canadian industry, however, with few exceptions, spends much less than other countries on training as a proportion of payroll.)

The system may be lovely but the results are horrible. The high-school dropout rate is about 30 per cent; 28 per cent of young people born here are functionally illiterate and 40 per cent innumerate. Some graduates need retraining to qualify for entry-level jobs.

With new highs in unemployment and under-employment associated with poor or useless skills, we are haemorrhaging treasure as well as blood.

Canada has been a world leader for at least 25 years in telecommunications and educational TV, which can provide quick, universal access to information and knowledge. We can revamp our systems to exploit current digital interactive technologies - to enable students to question the teachers - and provide lifelong learning.

Doing it would save money, boost competitiveness, stimulate growth and develop a trained workforce. But no government has taken any such action.

In Japan, Korea, Singapore, Thailand, Malaysia and Hong Kong, technology is being fully exploited by governments and business for education and training. The European Community...aims to increase the use of telecommunications for education with technology ranging from E-mail to satellite links.

The United States is even more ambitious, with a national plan for local learning and delivery systems, an invisible interstate electronic highway of information networks.

It is downright galling to see other countries beat us to the punch like this. None of this calls for megabucks, since the technological infrastructure and much of the software are already in place. It would save tax dollars. It's essentially a rechanneling for better use of what we already have, a united effort to solve our problems together and construct a culture of competence. But that requires immediate, energetic action and commitment.

From a speech by Bernard Ostry, former federal deputy minister of communications

Clearly, however, today's learning environment demands more than this. Canadians are increasingly choosing American schools because they feel the quality of instruction may be higher, or the variety of courses greater, or the scientific facilities better. There is also the question of contacts: if we're part of North America, where should the North American elite go to get educated? No reason they couldn't choose Canada, the way many still choose Switzerland — but we don't seem to be interested or interesting enough to promote the volume or quality of exchanges our trading relations suggest we merit. Canada's a splendid place to visit, but there's no reason you should have to come here just to go to a Canadian school or university. With new technology, we could be offering courses throughout North America.

Perhaps the most intriguing effort to increase teaching productivity has been the emergence of so-called "executive" programs, cost-covering short courses for candidates backed by their companies. Accompanying these have also been shorter professional development courses. These may last two or three days, or perhaps a week, and are designed to summarize the state of the art on particular management functions, such as marketing, exporting, new financial services, etc.

Despite these programs, private companies are increasingly moving away from university suppliers to search out private sector suppliers and even to do more training in-house as part of the on-going efforts to build team work and corporate culture as added bonuses of the learning experience. More and more companies have their own training centres, for example. Some companies have bought up failed private universities and converted them into corporate training centres. These centres increasingly use computer-based technology and multimedia technology for creating course content, thereby achieving the uniform and reliable standard of presentation together with corporate relevance that were always question marks with university providers. Ironically, many university professors are part of those company education networks, as are some broker services supported by provincial governments.

T hus, for management, and for some technical professionals, business has begun to create a continuous learning environment tailored to its needs and rhythms, using external expertise from universities, consulting firms and other sources, according to choice. For better or worse, these changes are in effect destroying the monopoly of universities and professional schools as society's sole source of expertise and reducing their market shares. Gradually, with or without commitment to greater choice, the same process will erode the system of public and even private schools. What this shows is that the permanent learning society is a reality on the demand side, even if it needs work on the supply side. The bottom line is that if Canadian educators don't make up their minds to serve their natural markets, someone else will.

To be sure, students have always had other educational options. But now we're living in a global marketplace. They can have other options worldwide. Those options are likely to increase dramatically over the next 10 years. Already there are eight universities offering distance learning programs in North America. But in Canadian practice, distance learning is almost always a poor cousin to the perceived main priorities of the institution.

Researchers explain the lack of link-up in schools, despite the contrary rush to networking in the private sector, as a combination of resource constraints, technological illiteracy on the part of teachers and curriculum ties. Additionally, and conditioning everything else, is the powerful force for democratization that computer link-ups bring. Teachers may or may not be in favour of the downward power shift computers bring to society: they rarely wish it for their own classrooms.

There are some encouraging pilot programs, however. Some school boards are beginning to incorporate learning networks into their curricula. The North York School Board, using Internet and SchoolNet, a federal program, will have a number of its schools working on networks within the year. You can get an idea of the power of this service by checking out the SchoolNet bulletin board on the Ottawa FreeNet. AT&T Learning Network, a commercial service, has some 30 Canadian schools. KidsNet, an international program based on Internet, is well developed and easy to access. Attached to this chapter is a discussion of that project together with instructions for participating along with a reference number. Although the report is a year out of date, we think it provides a vivid demonstration of what these programs can accomplish. Interestingly, the Canadians behind KidsNet turned their attention to a national program that links children across Canada including remote northern communities in a project that explores native cultures. It's called KIDS FROM KANATA. A call to the Canadian reference in the report below will bring you in touch with those details. Other children's forums include, besides "KIDLINK", "CANAM", and "KIDSPHERE".

The fact is that there is now no real reason to deny our children the advantages of undertaking collaborative projects with their peers around the world. The real technical obstacles come down to the discomfort of many teachers with the technology and the simple fact that very few school classrooms have an outside phone line. These are hardly reasons for leaving schools out of the networking that is reconfiguring the material life of the country.

Again, the bottom line is the same. We have the technology. Whether we have the will to use it to serve public goals is the real question.

If you're fed up with school inertia, you can get involved yourself. The following explains how. . .

The KIDS-92 Newsletter
A Global Dialog for Children 10-15 Years

Issue Number 1, June 10, 1991.

KIDS-92

KIDS-92 is a grassroot project aiming at getting as many children in the age group 10 -15 as possible involved in a GLOBAL dialog. The project will continue until May 18th 1992.

In its simplest form, the dialog will be an exchange of personal presentations and views on the desired future of this world. The means of communication may be ordinary mail, fax, video conferencing, hamradio, or whatever.

We hope that your children be allowed to participate more fully, so that they can join the other kids in the ongoing global discussion using electronic mail.

THE FIRST STEP: The Personal Presentation

Meetings between people usually start by the participants introducing themselves. The same is required by children participating in KIDCAFE and KIDS-ACT, which are 'where' the children meet to talk using electronic mail or other forms of electronic communication.

We want each kid to introduce himself/herself by answering the following four questions:

1) Who am I?

2) What do I want to be when I grow up?

3) How do I want the world to be better when I grow up?

4) What can I do now to make this happen?

THE SECOND STEP: The Discussion

The dialog takes place day and night on different conferencing systems, BBS systems, computer networks, and through individual electronic mailboxes. KIDS-92 is not a file area on a computer's hard disk. It's a process.

To enable communication between people across borders in our 'global village', we administer several 'discussion lists' on a computer in North Dakota, USA. A discussion list is simply an address list for electronic mail. A message sent to the list called KIDCAFE, will automatically be forwarded to all the addresses on this mailing list.

Through these lists a vivid discussion can take place using ordinary electronic mail. Each message sent to the lists is redistributed to a large number of mailboxes (and conference systems) world-wide.

We currently have the following discussion lists:

RESPONSE is where the children send their responses to the four questions. This is the only purpose of this list. When this is done, we invite them to send messages to KIDCAFE and KIDS-ACT.

KIDCAFE is for kids aged 10 - 15. Here, they can talk about whatever they like, find new friends in other countries, discuss the future, school, hobbies, environment, or whatever. Only those at the correct age can write messages to KIDCAFE, and they need to send their personal introductions to RESPONSE before starting.

KIDS-ACT is for kids aged 10 - 15. Here, they can talk about what THEY can do NOW to achieve their future visions. The rules for participation is as for KIDCAFE.

KIDS-92 is for teachers, coordinators, parents, social workers, and others interested in KIDS-92. This is where we post information about important developments, exchange experiences, report media coverage, news, etc.

KIDS-91 is where KIDS-91 is currently being reviewed. Later this year, KIDS-91 will be closed and turned into a read-only history database. The archives of KIDS-91 contains interesting information for teachers and others.

KIDPLAN is for those who want to participate in the planning of the project.

Subscriptions to all lists are free for everybody.

The KIDS-92 celebration is planned to take place on May 18-19, 1992.

During those days, the children will be invited to "chat" with each other in a global electronic dialog, and to participate in other technological experiments.

HOW TO PARTICIPATE IN KIDS-92

You can choose to participate in KIDS-92 with "your" children in many ways:

Level 1: Ordinary Mail!

Level 2: One-Way Electronic Mail

Level 3: Online - Participative

Level 4: Online - Full Interactive Communications

Level 5: Online - Interactive and Planning.

Level 1: Send By Ordinary Mail!

Have the kids respond to the four questions. Note: Each response should contain the child's FULL name, age and city/place (as the last phrase of the response)!

Save the responses on computer diskettes (MS-DOS 5.25" or 3.5" or Macintosh) as ordinary DOS or ASCII text files (text written with WordPerfect is also acceptable). Write the text with left margin 0 and right margin 60 to make it easy for the organizers to send it to the global data base.

On the top of the file, write the teacher(s) names, the class name, the school name and mailing address. Add your electronic return address, if you have one.

We strongly urge you to send the responses in electronic form! This is the only way that we can be sure that we enter the student's names correctly. This is also the only way that we can guarantee that their responses will end up in the global data base.

Mail the diskette(s) to

KIDS-92, 4815 Saltrod, Norway (Europe)

Or, send by telefax to phone number: +47 41 27111

If you are sending handwritten responses, please write the names clearly using Latin block letters.

Level 2: Online - One-Way Electronic Mail

You need access to a computer, a modem, a communication program, and an electronic mailbox for international electronic mail.

If this sounds mysterious to you, start by reading a book on communication. How you get access to electronic mail varies by country. The easiest way may to contact a local University or Research Organization and ask if they could let you have a mailbox for KIDS-92.

If this doesn't get you anywhere, try to find a BBS (Bulletin Board System) connected to FidoNet. These systems generally give everybody cheap access to global electronic mail. [For addresses contact the Canadian Representative listed below]

Level 3: Online - Participative

You can "subscribe" directly to the mailing list through Internet and associated networks. The alternative is to use participating mailbox/conferencing systems. . . .

Level 4: Online - Full Interactive and Communications

Read and respond to all KIDS-92 topics online. Read and enter responses to the four questions directly. Send private electronic mail to other participants - form 'keypals' relationships with new friends.

Let the students participate in regular online 'chats' with other children. For example, through KIDCAFE or KIDS-ACT. Encourage them to explore the world with the new tools, and to use KIDS-ACT for more serious talk.

Regularly print out messages from RESPONSE, KIDCAFE, and KIDSACT. Post the printout on the wall, publish it in daily newspapers, or make it available for all participants in other ways. Use the information in geography, environmental studies, history, and other classes.

Level 5: Online - Interactive and Planning

Join KIDPLAN and become a member of the KIDS-92 staff of volunteers. Join by sending a message to listserv@vm1.nodak.edu with the following command in the TEXT of your message: SUB KIDPLAN Your-first-name Your-last-name. . . .

FOR MORE INFORMATION

Canada:

Jonn Ord: Email: Jonno@scinet.UUCP
SciNet/SciLink, 339 Wellesley Street, East, Toronto, Ontario
Phone: 416-922-7001

Skill Training in Remote Communities

Here's the problem: 18,000 people live in remote communities scattered across 3,000 kilometres and three time zones of the Canadian Arctic. It is both physically impossible and financially improbable to offer skills training with the current system of education. [During the recent federal election, Nunavut residents were neither visited nor canvassed by politicians. CBC North offered free time broadcasts — no one took them up. Authors' note]

It is also horrendously expensive to bring people out of remote communities for training. The impact of separation on family members trying to arrange care for children if forced to leave is another consideration. The Inuit population has only 10 university graduates; a majority of teen-agers do not complete high school because of the problems of distance and isolation.

The self-government agreement and land-claims settlement that will bring a new Nunavut government across the Central and Eastern Arctic by 1999 have created a crucial need for qualified Inuit managers to fill the estimated 1,000 new jobs to be created.

Here's the solution: Interactive televised satellite instruction. Atii ("Let's go!" in Innu) Training Inc., a non-profit Inuit agency, has a one-year pilot project designed to bridge the vast Arctic and generate the management training skills Inuit will need to take charge of a coming new territorial government.

Lessons originating in the Inuit Broadcast studio in Iqaluit are bounced off a satellite to seven classrooms where students - many of them already involved in supervisory or low level management positions - use a telephone hook-up to ask questions or respond to assignments. The classrooms are supervised by community teacher aides.

The pilot project is a collaboration with several colleges, a board of education and a communication system. It goes beyond the bounds of Nuvavut to two Inuit communities in Quebec, one in Labrador and the Innu (Indian) community of Sheshatshui. Management training examples are adapted to northern situations. Buying television time on TVNC (a private northern television network, will cost about $300,000. The equivalent cost of delivering the same training through conventional classes would cost millions.

From the files of *The Globe and Mail*

11

How to Recycle Health Care

The comprehensive
Canadian health care
system dates back only to
1967, when governments
began picking up the tab for
doctors' visits and drugs. It
was only 10 years before
that governments began to
cover hospital costs. Thus
Canada's medicare program
is relatively young — just a
little over a generation.

True, it's enormously expensive: $60 billion a year in current dollars if you take into account everything. And it's growing.

However, when figured per head of population and in constant 1986 dollars, Canada's medicare system costs have remained remarkably stable. In contrast to the other big ticket items that make up government spending, Canada's medicare programs have remained relatively steady, rising from around $300 a head in 1967 to about $800 a head in 1990.

For comparison's sake, outlay on social services in those same constant dollars per capita has risen from about $700 a head in 1967 to around $2,200 a head in 1990, servicing the public debt from less than $100 a head to $2,000 over the same period, education from $700 a head to $1,000 a head, and everything else from $1,000 to $2,500.

What's been pushing up costs? Two factors account for 95 per cent of the rising real costs of health care: population growth, i.e. more people, and more service per capita, that is, more visits to the doctor. More people making more use of the system.

A possible explanation of this could be plague or killer bees: but there's been no plague. In fact, over the same period, the average life expectancy of Canadians and most other general health indicators have improved. Using the health care system makes us healthier.

Clearly, if the health care system were a business instead of a government program, we would say it's been a howling success — more people making more use of your service is just what you want to see as a business person. And if your customers are better off as a result, well, you should take a bow.

So why are we worried about health care? Clearly because of the failure of the public sector to perform in other areas. Without the debt charges, we wouldn't be squeezed on health care. Without the expansion of social services, we wouldn't be worried about health care.

Of course, we aren't paying in constant dollars, we're paying in current dollars. General inflation adds about 50 per cent to the current costs of health care over and above the other two factors. So while the system is actually doing pretty well, general inflation (not inflation of medical costs) masks that success by pushing costs up anyway. But government policy over that same 20 years, not the health care system, is responsible for that inflation.

So why is paying for health care suddenly such a big deal? Why all the talk of user fees [ostensibly to cut back on visits] and limited care [clearly to cut back on procedures]? One reason is that they sound good to people who don't know any better. Dr. Robert Evans of the University of British Columbia and the author of BC's health care reform package, says "user fees are the price we pay for stupidity." Yet clearly if user fees are going to make a difference, they will have to discourage some necessary treatment, thus tiering the system into those who can and can't pay. And clearly setting quotas or other limits on the number of procedures a patient can receive makes no sense either — if your child gets earaches, what doctor is going to say, "Sorry, you're only allowed three a year, so I can't treat this one..."

As for other bright schemes, like reducing hospital beds and increasing ambulatory care, the numbers show that increased service per capita in ambulatory care and pharmaceuticals already represents the fastest growing segments of health care costs. More patients are being treated as outpatients and drugs are already replacing surgery. Once again, the system works. So why are we trying to fix it?

Clearly, if we want to streamline costs, there is only one avenue that will be productive: get more done for less cost during the visits people make now. Already, as anyone knows who's been to hospital, a lot has been done in this area. Nurses and paramedics are doing a lot more, doctors are focusing their time on the points where their expertise is the most valuable — diagnostic or skilled treatment, such as surgery.

Do-it-yourself home health tests are soon to become a multi-billion-dollar industry. There are now many more types and suppliers of home health test for diagnosis and monitoring of more varied medical conditions; measuring a greater variety of symptoms and indicators; attaining greater levels of accuracy; and costing proportionately less than even a few years ago. Growing by 18% a year, annual sales of home testing kits may top the $2 billion mark by 1995.

Some of the more popular home tests include those for diabetes ($250 million in annual sales in the most recent 12 month period); pregnancy ($150 million); ovulation ($17 million); urinary tract infection and colo-rectal cancer.

Thanks to recent breakthroughs in biotechnology, the next year or two should see the unveiling of tests to detect strep throat; nutrient deficiencies; sexually transmitted diseases; alcohol and drug abuse; cholesterol levels.

Franchises are now being marketed in Canada and the United States which offer do-it-yourself diagnoses, prescription pickup and video viewing of health or disease issues in which you're interested, while you wait.

From the files of *Futurescan*

Still, there's room for improvement. But the fastest way to get there is to use markets to control costs within fee caps. And to find a way to promote networks as a mid-way point between hospitals and markets. So better telecommunication links between urban centres and remoter communities, using technology hubs for economies of scale and scope, breaking up provincial boundaries to profit from spare capacities within the national system, to name just a few opportunities.

Better use of neighbourhood clinics to take heat off emergency rooms would produce savings. Better use of technology to improve diagnosis.

There are also administrative savings to be had from such things as "smart" health cards (that is, a card much like a bank card with an electronic chip that allows you to carry your entire medical history in your wallet), and paperless records systems from admission to discharge. No one denies that better hospital management could improve productivity and use of existing computer systems.

MDs Threaten to quit over new computer system:

Hospital doctors, dentists and pharmacists threatened to quit unless the hospital agreed to slow down its implementation of a computerized records system. They also called for a supervisory panel of doctors, nurses and other hospital professionals to oversee implementation of the system.

Problem: The system, which displayed a patient's medical records, test results and other data, responded too slowly, the medical professionals complained. Unanimous consent of the panels would be necessary before the system could be used in treatment units, including the emergency ward. An agreed upon guideline: the system had to produce the required information within four seconds.

Computer Files Need Better Safeguards

Quebec's privacy watchdog gave the province's hospitals three years to tighten up the safeguards on access to patients' files. The ruling followed a number of complaints of employees breaching security of medical data. Bringing systems into compliance with the binding guidelines (which include developing access codes that determine levels of access based on need to know): $1 million.

From the files of the *Montreal Gazette*:

Another area of reform is in the financing techniques used to pay for the system. By using governments as the managers of the insurance system, we are essentially creating a tax-funded system. This needlessly drives a wedge between the productive, private sector and the government-provided service. There is a way to take these programs off the government books and render them relatively self-financing, using the portfolio management techniques developed by the financial community during the 1980s.

Premium streams coming into the system from taxpayers should be invested in productive growth against future larger payouts caused by an ageing population, just like a mutual fund. Currently, the public sector money transferred into the health care system receives no yields but the real outlays double every 15 years. That's a real rate of return of more than 14 per cent. Capturing this for application to the system would delay the need for higher premiums.

Still, there are those who say that this will not get at the root problem of people making more and more trips to the doctor, especially as the population ages. Those criticisms are probably right. The real secret to saving the health care system is in fixing up the other elements of our national economy. We can slash the demand for social services by improving the ability of people to find work. We can end the tyranny of debt service by paying it off. And we can stop the erosion of living standards by becoming more productive and effective in world markets.

A good place to start: eliminating the constraints on making full use of the technology we already possess.

American physicians and investors alike are taking a microscopic look at electronic data interchange networks as a way to slice a sizeable chunk off the nation's $80 billion annual health care administrative costs.

Electronic networks, which reduce the paperwork associated with filing insurance claims, have succeeded in automating physicians offices and hospitals since last June, when the Bush Administration introduced legislation to encourage development of the technology.

Physician Computer Network (PCN) lets doctors communicate electronically, not only with managed-care providers and insurers, but also with clinical laboratories and hospitals.

PCN leases a computer system to physicians, including IBM hardware, software installation, training, service and upgrades, for about $3,000 a year—a third of what it would normally cost to automate a medical practice. Physicians also agree to spend up to 90 minutes a month viewing commercials and mailgrams, and completing research surveys from pharmaceutical companies that pay PCN for the exposure.

Through PCN, physicians can forward claims electronically to Medicare, Medicaid, Blue Cross/Blue Shield, the top 250 commercial carriers and 40 managed-care plans. "Physicians can get a one-time cash-flow improvement of $30,000 to $50,000 by reducing days outstanding from nine to 18 weeks for a paper claim vs. one to three weeks for an electronic claim," says Jerry Brager, CEO of PCN.

Physicians can also perform diagnostic tests via PCN, look up lab test results and change medications and orders for hospitalized patients.

"I no longer fill out 400 to 600 forms a month: What once took us a week, now takes a half-hour," says Dr. Neil Adelman, a general/internal medicine physician in Millburn. "The savings to me personally have been thousands of dollars."

Electronic data networks can assist in cutting health care costs in other areas. For example, if small or medium-sized companies could track the group data of a large insurance company's recorded hospital-based illnesses such as premature births or spinal injuries, they could better assess the needs of their own employees and provide in-house preventative programs that may cut down on future claims.

From the files of the *BUSINESS JOURNAL OF NEW JERSEY*

The next two chapters deal with some of

Canada's Regulated Industries

Heavily regulated industries are an artifact of the political process. If that process is flawed, then it is only logical that industry structure will be less than optimal. During the last 10 years, the political process grappled with, but failed to control government borrowing and constitutional reform. At the same time, the regulatory process also attempted to grapple with the changes affecting our two most important services — financial services and telephone and cable TV. In both cases, the main pressures for change sprang from the two forces driving almost everything else — technology and globalization. In each case, our regulatory authorities managed to accommodate a certain amount of change, all of which was hyped as preparing Canada for the global, information age. Yet in fact the changes left the industry more protected than ever from those trends, better able to resist them, and less pressured to adjust.

In the case of financial services, Canadians found themselves offered state-of-the-art convenience, but not offered outward looking financial, especially derivative, products. In the case of telephone and television, the Canadian industry remained isolated from — some authorities say 10 years behind — the great changes occurring in its major trading partner, the United States. There, a vast restructuring is laying the foundations for a completely new industry that combines video, voice and data on the same household line.

The regulatory changes thus protect the short-term interests of the major suppliers. The real price has been paid not so much by consumers of these services, but by Canada itself, in terms of the opportunity costs that come with being legislated into strategic followership. Ultimately, in the case of telecommunications, a great industry in which we have enjoyed a comparative international advantage may have been fatally wounded by this

12

Financial Services

Until the mid-1980s,
Canada's financial services
were regulated according to
a concept known as the
"four pillars". The four
pillars were the different
types of financial activity —
the chartered banks which
engaged in deposit taking
and lending, trust compa-
nies, investment dealers
and insurance companies.

Technology (chiefly computers linked buy phone) and the practice known as securitization (by which computers transform a large number of small debts into a small number of large assets) fused all the pillars together. Operationally, the distinction between a mortgage, a long-term deposit, a retirement mutual fund and a life insurance policy became increasingly hard to make. Like it or not, the businesses the four pillars sought to keep separate, were driven closer and closer together.

Eventually, after the United Kingdom executed the so-called "big bang" in which banks and investment dealers were allowed to join forces, and under pressure from provinces whose own regulations were increasingly liberalizing, federal authorities went ahead and changed the Bank Act to recognize the obsolescence and impracticability of the four pillars formula. Result: Canadian banks were allowed to acquire investment dealers and trust companies. And during the mid 1980s, Canada's largest investment dealers came under the ownership of the chartered banks. That was followed in the early 1990s by the absorption of Canada's largest trust companies.

Was this just prudent adjustment to the evolutionary trends in a vital industry? Or was the re-regulation also a cover for a rescue of investment dealers and trust companies hard-pressed by the turbulence of markets whose underlying characteristics were changing rapidly?

Despite the high price paid for investment dealers, it was a long time before they lived up to their promise once inside the banking framework. As for the trust companies, one of the most important of these, The Royal, was taken over by Canada's largest chartered bank in a shotgun marriage born of financial troubles.

Other trusts, like the Montreal Trust, owned by BCE, were also rumoured to be in difficulty owing to their commitment to real estate assets. The insurance industries, exempted from these buyouts at their own insistence, found themselves obliged to rescue one of their members, the Société des Coopérants, in the first insurance company insolvency in Canadian history.

Despite the headlines these events inspired, they represented a smooth Canadian adjustment, and contrasted sharply with US experience, where failure to reform financial regulations left the savings & loan institutions (roughly equivalent to Canadian trust companies) exposed and ultimately devastated — the largest financial failure in post-Depression banking history. The failure of the US to follow its other trading partners in permitting the blending of investment dealers and banks had another effect as well. It upset the hopes of Canadian banksers for the Canada-US Free Trade Agreement.

Under the FTA, Canadian banks have the right to establish themselves in the U.S. — that is, they can set up without discrimination. But they also have to conform to US regulations which prevent the kinds of combinations they only recently made at home. Other laws grandfathered the presence of Canada's big banks in the U.S. But in practice having the investment dealers in the family mean the banks are excluded from retail banking services, the particular area where Canadian banks excel. Until the US agrees to permit national branch banking and to allow banks to own investment dealers, Canadian banks will be effectively excluded from competing fully in the US.

This has had the effect of turning competition inward to the domestic market in Canada. As a result, Canadian banks are competing harder and harder for a share in the relatively small Canadian domestic market. This has been good for the consumer insofar as conventional banking services are concerned: banks are open longer, we can now bank by phone and, if we don't yet have full service banking, we can nevertheless handle securities transactions through the same organization.

So Canadian banks are effectively blocked from providing basic services in the US. (An exception is cash withdrawals from automatic teller machines. You can use a US ATM to withdraw money from your Canadian account.)   By the same token, US banks are effectively blocked from entering the Canadian market. The big Canadian banks are effectively protected from takeover by ownership rules. This law limits the smallest number of shareholders to 10 and the investment share of foreigners to 25 per cent. That means Canadian banks cannot be bought out, either by one of their own, or by a big international bank (one shareholder), or controlled by non-Canadians.

Investment rules also ensure that the Canadian public must use Canadian banks to do business in this country. The FTA permits US banks to book loans in Canada, but a Canadian withholding tax takes all the profit out of that business by ensuring that no US bank could lend in Canada at competitive rates. And just to seal the border tight, investment rules on tax free Canadian pensions require that 80 per cent of the portfolios be invested in Canada. Finally, to keep things really leak-proof, Canadian investors in foreign funds get no foreign tax credit on taxes levied by the home countries of those funds. More. The Canadian banks are also adept at excluding their foreign competitors from the bank clearing system and from the Interac bank card network. The upshot is that the retail banking market — the heart and soul of Canadian banking — is effectively sealed at the border. Who wins and who loses? The banks as a whole win, because this policy ensures that they have the Canadian short term deposit market all to themselves. For reasons we'll mention in a minute, that may be a rather hollow victory. The Canadian government wins, because these policies ensure that for the most part Canadians have to pay the extra price of Canada's excessive government borrowing — essentially paying twice, once at tax time, and again through higher interest rates at the bank. The Canadian consumer loses because they are effectively denied access to international competitors.

Of course companies of medium to large size have an exemption all their own to these arrangements. Under recently adopted mutual recognition rules for equity transactions, Canadian companies can use the relatively simpler documents acceptable in Canada to raise equity capital in US markets. Not surprisingly, almost all the transactions under these rules have been north-south, bypassing Canadian dealers. What the Canadian banks gained on the consumer swings, they are losing on the much more attractive roundabouts. What the banks won by sealing off the Canadian border, therefore, is simply to lock in murderous competition for a relatively small market based on banking the old fashioned way. Where they are outclassed is by the fast-growing fee-for-service investment business in the world's largest financial markets. One way out would be for some Canadian banks to combine to form banks of world class size and compete vigorously in world markets from their Canadian base. Unfortunately, that exit is blocked by a deadly combination of taxes and rules. The industry artefact emerging from Canada's reform of financial markets thus condemns our banking sector to slow self-destruction in intensifying competition for the least attractive part of the banking business.

Unfortunately, the barriers by which the banks exclude outsiders are also the barriers facing Canadian small entrepreneurs who might want to launch a knowledge-based business. The Canadian banks feel they are doing a good job of providing low-cost, low risk loans based on real assets. They also feel that riskier loans based on industry specialization should be provided by other lenders. Unfortunately, however, Canadian financial services have no place for this kind of lender, who needs a wider, deeper market than Canada on its own can provide. Sealing the border thus ensures that the best Canadian ideas will be sucked southward — desperately wounding our ability to compete on innovation.

A solution: apply competition policy to break the clearing system cartel, lift the withholding tax and change the bank ownership rules to permit industry restructuring. Then Canadian entrepreneurs could more easily access the capital they need — and Canadian banks could grow large enough to develop industry expertise and move into more lucrative fee-for-service activity.

13

Telecommunications

As was the case with financial services before Canada's Little Bang blew away the four pillars, telecommunications regulation in Canada continues to enforce artificial separations that can no longer be justified — despite the fact that the government introduced and passed a new telecommunications framework in 1992.

As with financial services, the Canadian regulatory situation reflects — broadly — the best interests of the service providers, as they have historically imagined them to be.

When there was a monopoly of both long distance and local service, the monopoly carrier dreamed of sealing off the border and having Canada all to itself. Unfortunately, changing technology meant that would lead to the loss of their lucrative corporate supplier base, either through the shifting of company telecom centres to the US or through the bypass of Canadian networks, i.e. finding way to make calls through the US where it's cheaper.

After a long period of reflection, Canadian regulators permitted another Canadian company — Unitel — to compete in the long distance market, requiring the Stentor companies to grant access to the network. Although the monopoly companies strongly resisted competition, they in fact had anticipated that it would occur and they prepared for it by, among other ways, seeking a US partner to help them improve their client services. They settled finally upon AT&T's arch-rival, MCI. The AT&T response was immediately to acquire 20 per cent of Unitel, and replace its Northern Telecom technology with that of AT&T, in effect giving them management control. This effectively ended the sealed border strategy.

At the same time, unsurprisingly, the public position of the two groups changed: the former monopoly companies are now all for permitting full competition; Unitel is for stiffer regulation to level the playing field against the dominant, former monopoly carrier.

Ironically, Canada's major trade deals, the FTA and the NAFTA, seek to control cross border competition in basic services and encourage it in so-called "enhanced" services — everything from voice mail to multimedia.

Yet because of our telecommunications regulation, our border remains strangely sealed with respect to multimedia telecom services. That's because, unlike the US, Britain or Japan, our regulatory framework seeks to maintain a separation between cable TV and telephone services. Despite the fact that these companies are all in the business of moving information through pipes to self-selecting addresses, they are kept apart by rules that are based on entirely different concepts.

Cable companies are subject to all sorts of rules about what they show, one of which is minimum Canadian content — in practice, a boost to Canadian newscasters.

Telephone transmission is based on a common carrier approach — the phone companies are not responsible for anything carried over their networks — only the senders themselves are.

It is time to recognize that the Canadian content rules have done their job, declare victory and wrap 'em up. There is no Canadian content rule at the bookstore, the video store, the theatre, the newsstand or the computer terminal. Yet Canadian products flourish because audiences like them — around the world, not just Canada. New technologies are opening new markets which, in turn, will narrow the cost differences between production centres. What's more, maintaining healthy competition among the plethora of communications technologies is the best assurance that Canadians will be not priced out of their own communications networks.

The distinctions between telephone and cable are breaking down faster in the US than in Canada. The result has been to promote a series of takeovers and alliances between cable companies, entertainment suppliers and phone companies in the US, culminating in the multi-billion dollar merger of Bell Atlantic and Tele-Communications, Inc.(TCI). In effect, the US is rewiring itself to move a whole range of entertainment products still under development into the household — everything from video on demand to print-yourself news and education services.

Entertainment (including films, TV and videogames), news and education are industries in the $80 billion-$100 billion a year range. The US regional phone company annual revenues are around US$12 billion. The new company, Bell Atlantic-TCI, has combined revenues of US$15 billion. Clearly, even a 10 per cent share of the revenue flow of the other industries to be piped interactively into the home would could nearly double the annual revenues of the new enterprise. The boost to other alliances — e.g. US West Inc and Time Warner ($2.5 billion), Nynex Corp and Viacom Inc. ($1.2 billion)—could be even greater.

These represent sectoral shifts in the economy on the order of tectonic plates creating new continents. They promise to completely transform the parameters of material life in the US and create billions of dollars worth of business opportunities in the process. Thanks to our regulation patterns, Canadian companies remain completely excluded from this shift unless they can sell into the US. Canadian suppliers — and they include giants such as Northern Telecom and Newbridge Networks Corporation as well as production software houses like Alias and SoftImage are already doing this.

Media, communications and computer companies have been rushing into mergers and alliances to help them compete amid rapid changes in information technology. All are looking for a spot on the information highway, which will combine television, computers and telephones, giving people access to a vast new array of entertainment and data.

These deals fall into three basic categories — those dealing with the content, how the content is distributed, and how it manipulated in the home or office.

Some recent examples:

CONTENT

Warner Communications Inc.-Time Inc.- the first mega-deal to illustrate changes in communications. It brought together a major maker of movies and TV programs with a major publisher of printed information.

Viacom Inc. - Paramount Communications Inc.- the most sharply contested media company takeover. Viacom owns cable TV networks, cable systems, TV and radio stations. Paramount has movie and TV production, sports teams, cable networks, publishers. Rival bid comes from home shopping network QVC Network Inc.

DELIVERY

Bell Atlantic-Tele-Communications Inc.- this deal shatters the idea that information has to come either by telephone or by cable. The companies could reach more than 10 million consumers nationwide with combined systems.

AT&T-McCaw Cellular - the largest long distance company and the largest cellular company could speed deployment of wireless phoning to many more people and erase the barrier between local and long distance service providers.

US West and Time-Warner - ready to offer inter-active (two-way) services by phone, cable TV or both.

MANIPULATION

Intel-Microsoft — working on ways to link telephones to computers. And, with General Instrument Corp., they are developing a settop box to control interactive TV.

IBM Corp.-Apple Computer Inc.: several joint ventures to develop different kinds of multimedia devices. Multimedia combines text, audio and video.

Kaleida-Motorola Inc.-Scientific-Atlanta Inc.- developing a settop box to control interactive TV.

3DO Corp.- developing a chip and software set they intend to be a standard platform for games, interactive cable TV and other forms of consumer-oriented computing.

Every study of competitiveness shows that a robust domestic market is the best way to breed the excellence required to attack global markets. Bold changes in the rules would help Canada become a relative powerhouse in these new areas.

Regulating cable companies on a common carrier basis like phone companies would help facilitate the fusion of the technologies. One of the main beneficiaries would be Canadian culture, because it will enable Canadian input into the new generation of interactive products and services and ensure they can be produced, bought and sold in Canada.

Ending the division between cable and phone is only one part of the story, however. There is the distinction between local calling and long distance and between wired and non-wired telecommunication. The new technologies include satellite, and the construction of the new world-wide Iridium network, which will enable person to person communication anywhere on the planet — you have just one phone number and it works anywhere — and other, wireless technologies like cellular.

The advent of new computer products — so-called personal digital assistants, like Apple's Newton, etc. — mean that what is now mainly a voice network — cellular — will soon be carrying data, including graphics and video. In many parts of the world, wireless technology will be the technology of choice because of the expense of laying or replacing existing wires.

A federal study has concluded that telecommunications is of critical importance to most Canadian businesses, but also that Canada lags behind the United States in some areas of the industry. The study looked at customer service, cost control, product innovation, reduced product cycles — and found that most respondents felt that telecommunications affected their competitive position. Some were still waiting for services that have been available in the U.S. for some time. Some indicated that they had considered moving part of their telecommunications-intensive operations to the U.S. to take advantage of lower prices.

Canadian companies are concerned not only about price differences between Canada and the United States but with the rate at which services are deployed. The study included 65 small, medium, and large Canadian and U.S. companies in a variety of sectors.

From the files of an ROB Special Report

The effect of these developments will be to end the monopoly wired phone companies now have in local calls. Again, Canadian regulatory patterns create an artificial barrier to change by keeping local calls priced below cost through cross-subsidies from long distance service. The effect of these distortions is to inhibit competition in price and variety of long distance services and competition in technology for local services. Once again, the main victim is Canadian entrepreneurs who might otherwise be active in these new, growing areas. The short run gainers are the phone companies. But in the longer run, the rigidities in the current system mean they will be unable to keep up with US dynamism. So our duopoly must live under the constant threat of an eroding business customer base as companies use their networks to re-route telecommunications to minimize Canadian volumes.

Taken together these regulations, in financial services and telecommunications, show how the current Canadian political system has struggled, more or less unsuccessfully, with trying to force technological change to serve social goals established for a different age and different conditions. There may be a case for trying to force financial services into a certain pattern that preserves things as they were for as long as possible. There may be a case for thinking of telecommunications as an affair of copper-wired telephone systems totally distinct from other information systems, to which all Canadians should have access. These are social choices we are entitled to make.

"The corporate landscape is littered with the remains of once-formidable competitors who could not recognise structural changes...fast enough to capitalise on their windows of opportunity."
Raymond W. Smith, CEO,
Bell Atlantic

But trying to hold back change has never been a successful strategy and usually ends with the irrecoverable ruin of what the policy was designed to save. The time has come to recognize that our main regulatory agency in telecom and broadcasting, the Canadian Radio and Telecommunications Commission (CRTC), as currently conceived and organized, is a naked emperor guarding an empty safe. Interestingly, however, none of our trading partners (except New Zealand) has actually scrapped its CRTCs. Arguably, there is a case for its fusing its culture and telecommunications wings into one organization and developing a set of pro-competition regulations based on price caps as long as the industry contains players who could otherwise dominate markets. Price caps would remove inducements to cross-subsidize services. But the vast sweep of the CRTC's current mandate as well as its bifurcated perspective on its responsibilities must end if Canada is to remain a player in this dynamically evolving industry.

From the files of *THE FUTURIST, 01/01/93*
© World Future Society 1993,
By James Snider,

An Information Age Consumer Bill of Rights

In the summer of 1962, John F. Kennedy introduced a consumer bill of rights. Four rights were
mentioned: the right to safety, the right to be
informed, the right to choose, and the right to be
heard. . .The new vision would reflect the advances
in information technology since 1962.

The five rights are:

1. The right to be educated about product
   strengths and weaknesses.

2. The right to trust sources of product information.

3. The right to state-of-the-art information infrastructure that empowers consumers to efficient-
   ly use their time, money, and energy.

4. The right of all, whether urban or rural, rich or
   poor, to access the information infrastructure.

5. The right to privacy, preventing sellers and others from abusing personal information gained in
   product transactions.

14

THE CHALLENGE: CONNECT

This book is sending two signals. The first is that a dramatic change is reaching critical mass in the material life of Canadians. As the new, global information economy advances, a new productive organization is emerging to supersede the firm.

That organization is the network. The network is replacing the firm as the engine of entrepreneurship, the instrument through which economic growth is achieved. The second signal is that government urgently needs to adjust to this change.

The emergence of productive networks strengthens the intrinsic tendencies of the information economy:

- to empower individuals over hierarchies, the many layered "silos" of the industrial era;

- to empower the micro-economy over the macro-economy. This is especially important for Canada's current economic preoccupations.

For 10 years or more Canadians have been debating economic health in terms of the macro-economy—the size of government deficits and debts, whether money should be tight or tighter, how to get the growth rate up and the unemployment rate down, how to turn around our current account. For 10 years, various combinations have been tried and nothing much has changed at the macro level.

However important the macro economy may be, it does not make the machine go. It has become a dependent, rather than an independent, variable. The independent variable has become the micro-economy. And it is at the micro level where the really interesting changes are taking place.

This brings us to the book's second signal. Canada is currently hamstringing itself because its public sector institutions have so far failed to adjust to the emerging new reality of productive networks. In every sector, our government institutions and policies have successfully resisted matching the changes taking place in the private economy. Public power remains too centralized, departments too hierarchical. Government is too cumbersome and too expensive. Even more important, government's micro-economic policy focus is increasingly outdated.

The object of most government analysis remains the firm, not the network. In government's policy models, the economy is divided into neat categories: producers, consumers, the employed, the unemployed, competitors, economic equilibria, etc. None of this applies to the emerging world of networks.

There are few clear divisions on networks. Networks produce as they consume and vice versa. Networked individuals, organizations, groups, whatever, compete as they cooperate and vice versa. And, like the underground economy—itself a kind of network—the unemployed are employed and vice versa. Networks are about flows, sharing, cooperating, working together at the same time they are about competing, learning and teaching...None of the traditional analytical categories can meaningfully be applied. Indeed, the whole traditional government point of view is wrong: governments are not positioned above the network, all-surveying with the potential to control. With respect to networks, governments are like any other organization—they can participate or not.

Networks thus pose a challenge to all the traditional levers of public power. Governments today have four ways of changing our behaviour. They can persuade us with propaganda, bribe us with our tax money or that of others, fine us if we don't comply and failing that put us in jail. You can't persuade a network, it knows too much. You can't fine a network, it will bypass the collector; you can't jail it. You can't even pull the plug without running the economy in reverse. You can stimulate a network with some funds. That will increase traffic. But networks are about process, so the ends achieved may be different from those the policy-makers intended.

But there are other policy levers governments can use to participate in the changes now taking place around them. Those levers are what you'd expect for networks: connect, store, forward, and improve the management of client-server relations.

In practical terms, this means that governments have to make policy based on encouraging networks to form, helping networks interconnect when the unaided market will not (as in certain job shocks that trash existing networks so new ones have to be established). Government can act as a file server—the repository—for users of information which the government is legally mandated to collect and distribute. In short, governments can participate like any other network citizen. And, because they respond to different stimuli than some other organizations, governments can play a special role. Moreover, because networks have the ability to exclude free riders, networks overcome many of the objections to a positive government role.

For example, in the absence of an ability to tax, government programs could still circulate on the network as a kind of shareware. As a for instance: software for doing basic international market research as part of an export promotion plan.

Take unemployment. Perhaps one of the most intriguing uses of the network model is that it defines unemployment as network obsolescence. People become unemployed because they are no longer in touch with people who have jobs to distribute. Government intervention should simply help connect those people to viable networks where jobs can be found or, even better, where work can be done.

Another useful principle is that of the software writer's guide: let the client have as much (or little) control as s/he wants. Contract law and other rules governing business should be updated to accommodate networked relationships. But using these should be optional. Much of the effectiveness of a network comes from its self-enforcing characteristics. These promote flexibility and cooperation beyond the capacity of a legal system to enforce. At the same time there should be ways to protect intellectual property, say, or collect damages for unfulfilled contracts and having an appropriate legal framework in place would help. Moreover, such a framework would serve as a useful bridge leading to the legal provisions necessary to facilitate virtual corporations. (VCs are temporary companies that exist only as a network entity for the purpose of fulfilling a particular task, coordinated by telecommunications). Part of any such review should be competition policy to ensure that the kinds of cooperation networks encourage can in fact be carried on.

Canada's newly-elected federal government faces the enormous challenge of coming to grips with our changing ways of doing things. Perhaps the toughest test will be admitting that national macro-policy is really a thing of the past and that the future lies in transferring power to subsidiary levels of government, especially our cities. Among the economic ministries, one challenge will be learning to analyze networks and to promote non-proprietary connections that others control.

This book began by asking where to find the country's economic and political comfort zone. By now the answer should be clearer—it lies in accommodating our institutions to a networked economy. It lies in recognizing that while politicians continue to debate economic policy and constitutional arrangements, the private economy has been developing an organizational form that changes the debate's terms of reference.

Canada's electronic networking is now approaching critical mass. Many of those that are separate will soon join up. Beyond a certain threshold, which we appear to be reaching, this kind of interconnectivity quickly becomes self-generating. The failure of government to accommodate these changes already has palpable weight—measured in the lack of public confidence in schools, the declining value of MBA programs, the mushrooming of the underground economy, the shortcomings in telecommunications policy, the growing number of Canadian small firms listing on US stock exchanges. The way to move forward—the challenge facing those in public life especially is a double one:
1) Understand and accept that things have changed;
2) Catch up to the private sector's best practices in using imagination and available technology to do things differently. That's what's needed to get ahead and stay ahead of the changes dynamically transforming the world. That's what's needed to make Canada vibrant again.